ARTICLES OF WAR

1661, 1749 and 1866

ISBN 0-85937-275-8

Published by Kenneth Mason, Homewell, Havant, Hampshire

Produced in Great Britain by Articulate Studios, Emsworth

Articles of War

THE STATUTES WHICH GOVERNED OUR FIGHTING NAVIES 1661, 1749 AND 1886

by Dr NAM RODGER

Kenneth Mason

ISBN 0 85937 275-8

British Library Cataloguing in Publication Data

Articles of War 1661, 1749 & 1866.
1. Great Britain. Articles of War 1661
2. Great Britain. Articles of War 1749
3. Great Britain. Naval Discipline Act 1866
4. Great Britain, *Royal Navy*
5. Naval law – Great Britain
6. Great Britain. Navy – Regulations
I. Rogers, N A M
344. 103'14 KD128

ISBN 0-85937-275-8

Printed by Redwood Burn Limited, Wiltshire

Contents

by Dr NAM RODGER

Introduction

The *Articles of War* of the Royal Navy, with their ringing declaration that it is the Navy 'whereon, under the good Providence of God, the wealth, safety and strength of this Kingdom chiefly depend', are in principle among the best known of all the documents of naval history, but in fact the actual texts have hitherto been easily available only in those libraries with copies of the *Statutes of the Realm*, and the scope and purpose of the *Articles of War* are by no means as familiar as their name and preamble.

The first 'Act for the establishing Articles and Orders for the regulating and better government of his Majesty's Navies, Ships of War and Forces by Sea' was passed in 1661 by the first Parliament of the newly-restored King Charles II. The King had inherited from the Commonwealth the largest and most powerful fleet in Europe, recently victorious in wars against Spain and the Netherlands. The King was proud of his fleet, and knew and cared a great deal about it, but it presented him with considerable problems. The Navy had large debts which he had no means of paying off, and the allegiance of seamen long unpaid, and of officers originally chosen for their loyalty to the Lord Protector, was doubtful. Moreover the constitutional shifts and expedients of the Interregnum had produced no stable or effective system of naval administration. In his approach to these problems the King was guided by the advice of various officers, notably Sir William Penn, who had long experience of the Navy of the Commonwealth, and he pragmatically adopted and continued many of the policies of his predecessors.

The *Articles of War* of 1661 were the product of this approach, being founded very closely on those promulgated by Parliament on Christmas Day 1652, which in their turn owed something to the regulations of March 1648/9 established for the Parliamentary fleet under the command of the Earl of Warwick. The immediate cause of the issue of the 1652 *Articles* was the serious defeat by the Dutch which Blake's fleet had suffered off Dungeness that autumn, and in which, as he reported to the Council of State, 'there was much baseness of spirit'. Cowardice and indiscipline on the part of captains and flag officers was then, and was to remain for at least a century, one of the gravest weaknesses of the Navy, and the *Articles of War* were largely aimed at curbing them. Since the *Articles* are sometimes spoken of as a harsh penal code oppressing the wretched seamen, it is worth emphasising that they were originally concerned largely with the misdeeds of officers. The *Articles* of 1661 are in no sense a comprehensive penal code, but a haphazard assembly of regulations and admonitions, with a good deal of duplication and little order. They deal with such offences as drunkeness, quarrelling and swearing, desertion and sedition, theft from shipmates and from prizes, murder, sodomy and striking a superior officer – all of which were in those days at least as likely among the officers as the seamen. Other crimes were possible, or at least easy, only for officers; such were embezzling stores, dealing fraudulently with prizes or treacherously with the enemy, cowardice, negligence or disobedience in command of ships in action, misconduct in charge of convoys, wasting ammunition, and hazarding or burning one's ship. Only a single penalty, for sleeping on watch, seems to be mainly aimed at the common seamen.

The *Articles* of 1661 remained in force, with some amendment, for nearly ninety years. They were replaced by a new act in 1749, at the instigation of the Board of Admiralty then headed by Lord Anson. By this time the *Articles*, originally the only written instructions for the Sea Service, had been supplemented by the *Fighting Instructions* and the *Regulations and Instructions relating to His Majesty's Service at Sea,* commonly called the *Admiralty Instructions*. The former, issued in varying forms by successive commanders in chief of fleets and squadrons, later with the support of the Admiralty, gave increasingly detailed guidance to captains on their conduct in action, including the tactics they were to follow. The latter, first issued in 1731, provided a detailed code of rules for captains and their commissioned and warrant officers about the duties attached to their offices, especially about the care of stores and the keeping of accounts. These too were addressed to and chiefly concerned with the officers, but they included instructions to the captain on the discipline of the ship's company.

Both the *Fighting Instructions* and the *Admiralty Instructions* overlapped to some extent the *Articles of War*, but they did not replace them. Moreover the evils which had led to the original issue of 1652 had continued throughout the succeeding century. In the War of the Austrian Succession, which had just ended in 1749, cowardice and disaffection had been as prominent among captains and flag officers as ever before. In the principal naval action of the war, off Toulon in 1744, the second in command and most of his captains had refused to obey orders to come into action, and from a safe distance watched their superior fight a costly and indecisive battle against heavy odds. Moreover the courts martial provided by the *Articles of War* proved in this case, as they had in others, an ineffective measure. The severe penalties prescribed by the *Articles* were as often as not qualified by the phrase 'or such other punishment as the Court Martial shall see fit'. Under pressure from the accused's friends, political or otherwise, many courts martial saw fit to award very little punishment, or none at all.

Furthermore, sea officers were not in law, or to a considerable extent in practice, members of a permanent corps continually employed by the Crown. They accepted appointments to specific ships by specific commissions or warrants, during the tenure of which they were subject to court martial, but they could at any time resign and go onto half pay, when they at once ceased to be amenable to naval discipline. To resign in order to avoid a court martial was to forfeit the hope of future employment, at least until a change of ministry, but there were many well-connected and well-to-do officers for whom this prospect held few terrors.

To Anson and many of his contemporaries within and without the Service, it seemed to be imperative to strengthen naval discipline in order to remedy these evils. The revision of the *Articles of War* introduced into Parliament in 1749 proposed to do so mainly in two ways, by removing much of the liberty of courts martial to reduce the punishment for specific crimes, and to render half-pay officers liable to naval discipline. In addition there was a general revision of the wording of the *Articles*, and some further paragraphs covering contingencies not foreseen in 1661, together with regulations for the conduct of courts martial themselves.

The publication of the Admiralty's bill gave rise to a violent political storm, in which a strong minority of sea officers, mostly associated with the opposition groups gathered around the Prince of Wales, denounced it as tyranny. They particularly objected to the extension of the liability to court martial to officers on half pay. This would allow the Admiralty to compel an officer to accept any proferred employment, however disagreeable, degrading or dangerous it might be. There were many who suspected their political enemies of preparing to use this power to force them into commissions from which they were unlikely to return with profit, with honour, or perhaps at all.

So vigorous was the opposition that the Admiralty yielded, and the *Articles of War* of 1749 as passed made no provision for applying naval discipline to officers on half pay. In other respects, however, the new *Articles* were harsher and somewhat more comprehensive. Within a few years they were to be tested. During 1755 and 1756 Britain and France moved from unconcealed hostility to undeclared, and finally to open war. In the spring of 1756 Admiral the Hon John Byng sailed for the Mediterranean with a squadron to relieve the besieged fortress of Minorca. It was, at least in Byng's view, just such an appointment as the malcontents of 1749 had feared to be given. He considered his forces to be insufficient and ill-manned, and the task in any case impossible. He went expecting to fail, and not surprisingly, he did. After an indecisive action, pressed with no great enthusiasm, he returned to Gibraltar leaving Britain's most important overseas naval base to its fate. Sea officers, led by Anson, were furious; once more 'cowardice, negligence or disaffection' had brought disgrace on the Service and disaster on the country. The ministers in the Cabinet were equally aghast; they had lost a base of vital importance for the war, and the country, inspired by the opposition in and out of Parliament, seemed ready to blame them for the loss, unless they could fix the guilt on Byng. The admiral was court-martialled under the twelfth article, specifically acquitted of cowardice or disaffection, but convicted of 'failing to do his utmost' to destroy the enemy. As reworded, the *Articles* provided for only one penalty, and the court reluctantly condemned him to death. Many of the admiral's political friends deserted him, the King (who shared his officers' opinions to the full) refused a pardon. So the wretched Byng died to give courage to the others – and it must be said he did not die in vain, for this was almost (though not quite) the last case of its kind. Moreover in 1778, largely as a result of Byng's trial, the *Articles* were amended to permit courts martial to reduce many of the punishments at their discretion.

It was this amended version of the 1749 *Articles* which was in force at the time of the great mutinies of 1797, and some writers have fixed on them as a symbol of the harsh discipline to which they ascribe the mutinies. In fact, as we have seen, the *Articles* were concerned with indiscipline more among the officers than the men, and they did not in any case form part of the seamen's complaints (saving a vague demand for unspecified revisions made at the Nore). It is abundantly clear that the mutineers appreciated the need for strict discipline, and indeed employed it themselves. Their complaint was against low pay, and against arbitrary and capricious injustice, not sanctioned by the *Articles of War*, the *Admiralty Instructions*, or the law of the land.

The 1749 *Articles*, amended but not substantially changed, remained in force for more than a century. They carried into the midst of the Victorian era not a little of the spirit and the wording of the original regulations of 1652, and they were still largely concerned with misdeeds by officers many of which had ceased by the 1860's to be a serious problem, or even a possibility. Indeed the crimes of sea officers had long ceased to agitate the minds of public men as much as the welfare of seamen. The Admiralty was obliged by public concern, which to a great extent it shared, to take greater and greater care of its men, and to do so by ever more numerous regulations each of which further circumscribed a captain's liberty of action, and especially his liberty to punish as he thought fit. This too was in accordance with the approach of an age in which for the first time the government was interfering on a large scale in the lives of many of its subjects. In this new world the *Articles* of 1749 were an irrelevance. They were replaced by the *Naval Discipline Act* 1860 (23° & 24° Vic: c.123), which in its turn was replaced by those of 1861. 1864 (amended 1865), and finally by that of 1866, here printed, which summed up the earlier acts, and which remained in force until 1957.

The *Naval Discipline Act* 1866 was still generally known in the Service as the *Articles of War*, and it still repeated in its preamble that it is the Navy 'whereon, under the good providence of God, the Wealth, Safety and Strength of the Kingdom chiefly depend.' The arrangement, the approach and even the wording of the 1661 *Articles* were still plainly discernible. In spirit, however, the new Acts belonged to a different world. Taken in conjunction with the *Queen's Regulations & Admiralty Instructions*, they represented the final stage in the process by which centralised, legalistic naval administration had come to regulate in detail the internal affairs of the Queen's ships, and the daily lives of her officers and men. It was typical of the new *Articles* to prescribe in great detail how men might be punished, prisons organised, and courts martial regulated. In a sense, the 1866 *Articles* were as much concerned with the misdeeds of officers as those of 1661 had been, only the crimes to which they were addressed were quite different. Treachery and cowardice were not serious problems in the nineteenth-century Navy; cruelty and oppression aroused much less concern in the seventeenth. Once it had been all the authorities could hope for, and more than they could achieve, to keep admirals and captains to their duty; now they could regulate in detail the men's responsibilities to their officers, and the officers' to their men. In this the Navy's progress through successive editions of the *Articles of War* parallels the legal and constitutional progress of the country from an age in which the state was most alarmed by the threat of treason, to one in which it was most alarmed by the exploitation of the individual.

Charles II 1661

An Act for establishing Articles and Orders for the regulating and better Government of His Majesty's Navies, Ships of War, and Forces by Sea

13° Car. 11 St.1 c. 9(1661)

Articles to be observed

For the regulating and better Government of his Majesties Navies, Ships of War, and Forces by Sea; wherein under the good Providence and Protection of God, the wealth, Safety and Strength of this kingdom is so much concerned. Be it Enacted by the Kings most Excellent Majesty, with the advice and consent of the Lords and Commons in this Present Parliament assembled, and by the Authority thereof, That all and every the Articles and Orders in this Act mentioned, shall be duly and respectively put in Execution, observed and obeyed in manner hereafter mentioned.

I

The Publick Worship of God

That all Commanders, Captains, and Officers at Sea shall cause the publick Worship of Almighty God according to the Liturgy of the Church of England, established by Law, to be solemnly, orderly, and reverently performed in their respective Ships: And that prayers and preachings by the respective Chaplains, in holy Orders, of the respective Ships, be performed diligently; and that the Lords Day be observed according to Law.

II

Swearing Drunkenness, &c

Every person and persons in his Majesties pay, using unlawful and rash oaths, Cursings, Execrations, Drunkenness, Uncleaness, or other Scandalous Actions in derogation of Gods honour, and corruption of good manners, shall be punished by Fine, Imprisonment, or otherwise, as the Court Martial shall think fit.

III

Holding any Foreign Intelligence

If any officer, Mariner, Souldier, or other person in the Fleet, shall give, hold, or entertain intelligence, to, or with any King, Prince or State, being Enemy to, or any persons in Rebellion against his Majesty, his Heirs and Successors, without direction or leave from the Kings Majesty, the Lord High Admiral, Vice Admiral, or Commander in Chief, of any Squadron, every such person or persons so offending shall be punished with death.

IV

Letters or Messages from any foreign Prince, &c. Enemy to the King

If any Letter or Message from any King, Foreign Prince, State, or Potentate, being an Enemy to the Kings Majestie, his Heirs and Successors, or on their behalf, be conveyed to any Inferior Officer, Mariner or Souldier, or other in the Fleet, and the said officer, Mariner, Souldier, or other as aforesaid, do not within twelve hours having opportunity so to do, acquaint the Superior Commander with it; or if a Superior officer, or Mariner, being acquainted therewith by an Inferiour officer Mariner, or other, or himself in his own person, receiving a letter or message from any such Enemy or Rebel, and shall not in convenient time reveal the same to the Admiral, Vice Admiral, or the Commander of the Squadron, every such person shall be punished with death, or such other punishment as the Court-Martial shall think fit.

V

Relieving of any Enemy

No person or persons of the Fleet shall relieve an Enemy or Rebel, in time of War, with money, Victuals, Powder, Shot, Arms, Ammunition, or any other Supplies whatsoever, directly or indirectly, upon pain of death, or such other punishment as the Court-Martial shall think fit to impose.

VI

Papers, Charter Parties, &c. Taken in any Ship seised as prize

All the Papers, Charter Parties, Bills of Lading, Passports, and other Writings whatsoever, that shall be taken, seised, or found aboard any Ship or Ships which shall be surprised, or seised as Prize, shall be duly preserved, and not torn, nor made away, but the very Originals sent up entirely, and without fraud, to the Court of Admiralty, or such other Commissioners as shall be appointed for that purpose; there to be viewed, made use of, and proceeded upon according to Law, upon pain of loss of all the shares of the Takers, and such further punishment to be inflicted upon the Offenders therein, as the quality of their Offence and misdemeanor shall be found to deserve, and the Court-Martial shall impose.

VII

Prize, Ships or Goods seised for prize

None in his Majesties pay shall take out any Prize or Ship, or Goods seised on for Prize any money, plate, goods lading or tackle, before Judgement thereof first past in the Admiralty court, but the full and intire accompt of the whole, without imbeselment, shall be brought in, and Judgment past intirely upon the whole, without fraud, upon pain of such punishment as shall be imposed by a Court-Martial, or the Court of Admiralty; excepting, That it shall be lawful for all Captains, Sea-men, Souldiers, and others, serving as aforesaid, to take and to have to themselves as Pillage, without further or other accompt to be given for the same, all such goods and Merchandizes (other than Arms, Ammunition, Tackle, Furniture, or Stores of such Ship) as shall be found by them, or any of them in any Ship (they shall take in fight or prize) upon or above the Gun-Deck of the said Ship, and not otherwise.

VIII

Imbezelling Any Cables, Anchors, &c

None shall imbezle, steal or take away any Cables, Anchors, Sails, or any of the Ships Furniture, or any of the Powder, or Arms, or Ammunition of the Ship, upon pain of death or other punishment, as the quality of the offence shall be found by a Court-Martial to deserve.

IX

Foreign Ships taken as prize not making resistance

If any Foreign Ship or Vessel shall be taken as prize, that shall not fight or make resistance, that in that case, none of the Captains, Masters or Mariners, being Foreigners shall be stripped of their Clothes, or in any sort pillaged, beaten, or evil entreated, upon pain That the person or persons so offending shall forfeit double damages; but the said Foreign Ships, and all the Goods so taken, shall be preserved entire to receive judgment in the Admiralty Court, according to Right and Justice.

X

The Duty of Captains &c upon signal of fight. Not to yield or cry for quarter

Every Captain or Commander, who upon signal or order of fight, or view, or sight of any Ships of the Enemy, Pyrate, or Rebel, or likelihood of Engagement, shall not put all things in the Ship in a fit posture for fight, and shall not in his own person, and according to his place hearten and encourage the inferiour officers and common men to fight couragiously, and not to behave themselves faintly, shall be cashiered: And if he or they shall yield to the enemy, Pyrate, or Rebels, or cry for quarter, he or they so doing shall suffer the pains of death, or such other punishment as the offence shall deserve.

XI

All Officers shall observe the commands of the Admiral

Every Captain, Commander, and other Officer, Sea-men, or Souldier of any Ship, Frigot or Vessel of War, shall duly observe the Commands of the Admiral, or other his Superiour or Commander of any Squadron, as well for the Assailing or Setting upon any fleet, Squadron, or ships of the enemy, Pyrate, or Rebels, or joyning Battel with them or making Defence against them, as all other the Commands of the Admiral, or other his Superiour Commander, upon pain to suffer death or other punishment as the quality of his neglect or offence shall deserve.

XII

Officers that in time of fight shall Withdraw, or not fight

Every Captain, and all other Officers, Mariners, and Souldiers of every Ship, Frigot, or Vessel of War, that shall in time of any fight or engagement, withdraw or keep back or not come into the fight and engage, and do his utmost, to take, fire, kill, and endamage the Enemy, Pyrate, or Rebels, and assist, and relieve all and every of his Majesties Ships shall for such offence of cowardize or disaffection, be tryed and suffer pains of death, or other punishment, as the circumstances of the offence shall deserve, and the Court-Martial shall judge fit.

XIII

Officers and Ships appointed for Convoy, their Duty

The Captains, Officers, and Sea-Men of all Ships, appointed for Convoy and Guard of Merchant Ships, or any other, shall diligently attend upon that Charge, without delay, according to their Instructions in that behalf, and whosoever shall be faulty therein, and shall not faithfully perform the same, and defend the Ships and Goods in their Convoy, without either diverting to other Parts or Occasions; or refusing or neglecting to fight in their defence, if they be set upon or assailed, or running away cowardly, and submitting those in their Convoy to hazard and peril, or shall demand and exact any money, or other reward from any merchant or Master, for convoying of any

such Ships or other Vessels belonging to his Majesties Subjects, shall be condemned to make reparation of the damage to the Merchants, Owners and others, as the Court of Admiralty shall adjudge; and also be punished criminally according to the quality of their offences, be it by pains of death or other punishment, according as shall be adjudged fit by the Court Martial.
(It was a recent innovation to expect men-of-war to convoy merchantmen without fee.)

XIV

The penalty for not chasing an Enemy, or not relieving a friend

Whatsoever Person or Persons, in or belonging to the Fleet, either through cowardize, negligence, or disaffection, shall forbear to pursue the chase of any Enemy or Pyrate, or Rebel, beaten, or flying, or shall not relieve or assist a known friend in view, to the utmost of his power, shall be punished with death, or otherwise, as a Court-Martial shall find fit.

XV

Service commanded shall not be stopped or discouraged

When at any time, service or action shall be commanded, no man, shall presume to stop or turn backward or discourage the said service and action, by pretence of Arrears of Wages, or upon any pretence of Wages whatsoever, upon pain of death.

XVI

None shall betray their trust, nor yield to the Enemy

All Sea Captaines, Officers and Sea-men, that shall betray their trust, or turn to the Enemy, Pyrate, or Rebels, and either run away with their Ship or any Ordinance, Ammunition, or Provision to the weakening of the Service, or yield the same up to the enemy, Pyrates, or Rebels, shall be punished with death.

XVII

Deserting the service, or running away

All Sea Captains, Officers, or Mariners, that shall desert the Services or their Imployment in the Ships, or shall run away, or intice any others so to do, shall be punished with death.

XVIII

Spies

All persons whatsoever that shall come, or be found in the nature of Spies, to bring any seducing Letters or Messages from any enemy or Rebel or shall attempt or endeavor to corrupt any Captain, Officer, Mariner, or other of the Navy or Fleet, to betray his or their trust, and yield up any Ship or Ammunition, or turn to the enemy or Rebel, shall be punished with death.

XIX

Sedition, Mutiny

No person in or belonging to the Fleet, shall utter any words of Sedition or Mutiny, nor make or endeavour to make any Mutinous Assemblies upon any pretence whatsoever, upon pain of death.

XX

Concealers of trayterous or mutinous practices of words

No person in or belonging to the Fleet, shall conceal any Trayterous or Mutinous practices, designs, or words, or any words spoken by any to the prejudice of his Majesty, or Government, or any words, practices, or designs tending to the hinderance of the service, but shall forthwith reveal them to his superiour, that a meet proceeding may be had thereupon, upon pain of such punishment as a Court-Martial shall find to be just.

XXI

Quarrelling or striking a Superiour Officer None shall presume to quarrel with his Superiour Officer, upon pain of severe punishment, nor to strike any such upon pain of death, or otherwise, as a Court-Martial shall find the matter to deserve.

XXII

Unwholesomness of Victuals If any of the Fleet find cause of Complaint of the unwholesomness of his Victuals, or upon other just ground, he shall quietly make the same known to his Superiour, or Captain, or Commander in chief, as the occasion may deserve, that such present remedy may be had as the matter may require, and the said Superiour or Commander is to cause the same to be presently remedied accordingly; but no person upon any such or other pretence, shall privately attempt to stir up any disturbance, upon pain of such severe punishment as a Court-Martial shall find meet to inflict.

XXIII

Quarrelling or provoking speeches None shall quarrel or fight in the Ship, nor use reproachful or provoking Speeches tending to make any quarrel or disturbance, upon pain of Imprisonment, and such other punishment as the offence shall deserve, and the Court-Martial shall impose.

XXIV

Wastful expence of Ammunition That there be no wastful expence of any Powder, Shot, Ammunition, or other Stores in the Fleet, nor any imbezelment thereof, but that the Stores and Provisions be carefully preserved, upon such penalties by Fine, Imprisonment, or otherwise, upon the Offenders, Abetters, Buyers and Receivers, as shall be by a Court-Martial found just in that behalf.

XXV

Care of conducting and steering ships That care be taken in the Conducting and Steering of the Ships, that through wilfulness, negligence, or other defaults. none of his Majesties Ships be stranded or run upon any Rocks or Sands, or spit, or hazarded, upon pain, that such as shall be found guilty therein be punished by Fine, Imprisonment, or otherwise, as the offence by a Court-Martial shall be adjudged to deserve.

XXVI

Burning a ship All persons that shall willingly burn or set fire on any Ship, or Magazine, or Store of Powder, or Ship, Boat, Ketch, Hoy or Vessel, or Tackle or Furniture thereto belonging, not appertaining to an Enemy or Rebel, shall be punished with death.

XXVII

Sleeping upon Watch No man, in, or belonging to the Fleet, shall sleep upon his watch, or negligently perform the Duty imposed on him, or forsake his station, upon pain of death, or other punishment, as the circumstances of the case shall require.

XXVIII

Murthers All Murthers and wilful Killing of any person in the Ship shall be punished with death.

XXIX

Robbery and Theft All Robbery and Theft committed by any person in or belonging to the fleet, shall be punished with death, or otherwise, as the Court-Martial upon consideration of Circumstances shall find meet.

XXX

Provost Martial prisoners No Provost Martial belonging to the Fleet, shall refuse to receive or keep any Prisoner committed to his charge, nor suffer him to escape being once in his Custody, nor dismiss him without order, upon pain of being lyable to the same punishment which should have been inflicted upon the party dismissed, or permitted to escape, or such other punishment as the Court-Martial shall think fit.

XXXI

Apprehending offenders All Captains, Officers and Sea-men shall do their endeavours to detect, apprehend, and bring to punishment all offenders, and shall assist the Officers appointed for that purpose therein, upon pain to be proceeded against, and punished by the Court-Martial at discretion.

XXXII

Sodomy If any person or persons, in or belonging to the Fleet, shall commit the unnatural and detestable sin of Buggery or Sodomy with man or Beast, he shall be punished with death without mercy.

XXXIII

Misdeameanors and Disorders at sea All other Faults, Misdeameanors, and disorders committed at sea, not mentioned in this Act shall be punished according to the Laws and Customs in such cases used at Sea.

XXXIV

The Lords High Admirals power to grant Commissions to call Court Martials And it is hereby further enacted, That the Lord High Admiral for the time being shall by vertue of this Act, have full power and authority to grant Commissions to inferiour Vice Admirals, or Commander in Chief of any Squadron of Ships, to call and assemble Court-Martials, consisting of Commanders and Captains; and no Court-Martial where the pains of death shall be inflicted, shall consist of less than five Captains at least, the Admirals Lieutenant to be as to this purpose esteemed as a Captain; and in no case wherein sentence of Death shall pass by vertue of the Articles of aforesaid, or any of them (except in case of Mutiny) there shall be execution of such sentence of Death, without the leave of the Lord High Admiral, if the offence be committed within the Narrow Seas: But in case any of the offences aforesaid be committed in any Voyage beyond the Narrow Seas, whereupon sentence of Death shall be given in pursuance of the aforesaid Articles, or of any of them; then execution shall not be done but by order of the Commander in Chief of that Fleet or Squadron wherein sentence of Death was passed.

XXXV

Judge Advocate of any Fleet to administer an Oath for tryal of offence Court Martial

And be it further enacted and declared, That the Judge Advocate of any Fleet, for the time being, shall have full power and authority to administer an Oath to any person or witness in order to the Examination or Tryal of any of the offences aforesaid; and in the absence of a Judge Advocate, the Court-Martial shall have full power and authority to appoint any person to administer an Oath to the purpose aforesaid.

Proviso touching the powers of the Lord Admiral

Provided also, and be it further enacted by the authority aforesaid, That this Act, or any thing or things therein contained, shall not in any manner of wise extend to give unto the Lord Admiral of England for the time being, or to any of his Vice Admirals, Judge or Judges of the Admiralty, his or their Deputy or Deputies, or to any other Officers or Ministers of the Admiralty, or to any others having or claiming any Admiral Power, Jurisdiction or Authority within this Realm and Wales, or any other the Kings Dominions, any other power, right, jurisdiction, preheminence, or authority, then he or they, or any of them, lawfully have, hath, or had, or ought to have and enjoy before the making of this Act, other then for such of the offences specified in the several Articles contained in this Act, as hereafter shall be done upon the main Sea, or in Ships or Vessels being and hovering in the main Stream of great Rivers, onely beneath the Bridges of the same Rivers, nigh to the Sea, within the jurisdiction of the Admiralty, and in none other places whatsoever, and committed only by such persons as shall be in actual Service and Pay in his Majesties Fleet, or Ships of War.

(In eighteenth-century and later editions of the Statutes this paragraph is usually printed as a thirty-sixth article.)

George II 1749

An Act for amending, explaining and reducing into one Act of Parliament, the Laws relating to the Government of his Majesty's Ships, Vessels and Forces by Sea

22° Geo. 11 c.33 (1749)

Whereas the several Laws relating to the Sea Service, made at different Times, and on different Occasions, have been found by Experience not to be so full, so clear, so expedient or consistent with each other as they ought to be; For amending and explaining the said Laws, and for reducing them into one uniform Act of Parliament; Be it enacted by the King's most excellent Majesty, by and with the Advice and Consent of the Lords Spiritual and Temporal, and Commons, in this present Parliament assembled, and by the Authority of the same, That from and after the twenty-fifth Day of December one thousand seven hundred and forty-nine, an Act passed in the thirteenth Year of the Reign of King Charles the Second, intituled, An Act for establishing Articles and Orders for the regulating and better Government of his Majesty's Navies, Ships of War, and Forces by Sea; and also so much of an Act passed in the second Year of the Reign of King William and Queen Mary, An Act concerning the Commissioners of the Admiralty; as directs the Form of an Oath to be taken by every Officer present, upon all Trials of Offenders by Courts-martial, to be held by virtue of any Commission to be granted by the Lord High Admiral, or the Commissioners for executing the Office of Lord High Admiral; and also so much of an Act passed in the sixth Year of the Reign of King George the First, intituled, An Act for making perpetual so much of an Act made in the tenth Year of the Reign of Queen Anne, for the reviving and continuing several Acts of Parliament therein mentioned, as relates to the building and repairing County Gaols; and also an Act of the eleventh and twelfth Years of the Reign of King William the Third, for the more effectual Suppression of Piracy; and for making more effectual the Act of the thirteenth Year of the Reign of King Charles the Second, intituled, 'An Act for establishing Articles and Orders for the regulating and better Government of his Majesty's Navies, Ships of War, and Forces by Sea, as relates to the Trial and Punishment of Persons who shall commit any of the Crimes or Offences mentioned in the said Articles upon the Shore, in the Foreign Part or Parts; and also so much of an Act passed in the eighth Year of the Reign of King George the First, intituled, An Act for the more effectual suppressing of Piracy; as directs the Punishment to be inflicted by a Court-martial upon any Captain, Commander, or other Officer of any of his Majesty's Ships or Vessels of War, who shall receive on board, or permit to be received on board, any Goods or Merchandizes whatsoever, in order to trade or merchandize with the same (except the Goods and Merchandizes therein excepted) and also an Act passed in the eighteenth Year of the Reign of his present Majesty, intituled, An Act for the regulating and better Government of his Majesty's Navies, Ships of War, and Forces by Sea; and for regulating the Proceedings upon Courts-martial in the Sea Service; and also an Act passed in the twenty-first Year of the Reign of his present Majesty, intituled, An Act for further regulating the Proceedings upon Courts-martial in the Sea Service; and for extending the Discipline of the Navy to the Crews of his Majesty's Ships wrecked, lost, or taken; and for continuing to them their Wages upon certain Conditions, shall be, and the same are hereby repealed to all Intents and Purposes whatsoever.

2 Commencement of the Articles And for the regulating and better Government of his Majesty's Navies, Ships of War, and Forces by Sea, whereon, under the good Providence of God, the Wealth, Safety, and Strength of this Kingdom chiefly depend; Be it enacted by the King's most Excellent Majesty, by and with the Advice and Consent of the Lords Spiritual and Temporal, and Commons, in this present Parliament assembled, and by the Authority of the same, That from and after the twenty fifth Day of December one thousand seven hundred and forty-nine, the Articles and Orders herein after following, as well in Time of Peace as in Time of War, shall be duly observed and put in Execution, in Manner herein after-mentioned.

I

Publick Worship to be performed All Commanders, Captains, and Officers, in or belonging to any of his Majesty's Ships or Vessels of War, shall cause the publick Worship of Almighty God, according to the Liturgy of the Church of England established by Law, to be solemnly, orderly, and reverently performed in their respective Ships, and shall take care that Prayers and Preaching, by the Chaplains in Holy Orders of the respective Ships, be performed diligently; and that the Lord's Day be observed according to Law.

II

Penalty of profane Swearing, &c All Flag officers, and all Persons in or belonging to his Majesty's Ships or Vessels of War, being guilty of profane Oaths, Cursings, Execrations, Drunkenness, Uncleanness, or other scandalous Actions, in Derogation of God's Honour, and Corruption of good Manners, shall incur such Punishment as a Court-martial shall think fit to impose, and as the Nature and Degree of their Offence shall deserve.

III

Penalty of holding illegal Correspondence with an Enemy If any Officer, Mariner, Soldier, or other Person of the Fleet, shall give, hold, or entertain intelligence to or with any Enemy or Rebel, without Leave from the King's Majesty, or the Lord High Admiral, or the Commissioners for executing the Office of Lord High Admiral, Commander in Chief, or his Commanding Officer, every such Person so offending and being thereof convicted by the Sentence of a Court-martial, shall be punished with Death.

IV

of not acquainting the superior Officer with any Message from an Enemy If any Letter or Message from any Enemy or Rebel, be conveyed to any Officer, Mariner, or Soldier, or other in the Fleet, and the said Officer, Mariner, Soldier, or other as aforesaid, shall not, within twelve Hours, having Opportunity so to do, acquaint his superior Officer, or the Officer commanding in Chief, with it; or if any superior Officer being acquainted therewith, shall not in convenient

Time reveal the same to the Commander in Chief of the Squadron, every such Person so offending, and being convicted thereof by the Sentence of the Court-martial, shall be punished with Death, or such other Punishment as the Nature and Degree of the Offence shall deserve, and the Court-martial shall impose.

V

of Spies, and of delivering seducing Letters, &c

All Spies, and all Persons whatsoever, who shall come or be found, in the Nature of Spies, to bring or deliver any seducing Letters or Messages from any Enemy or Rebel, or endeavour to corrupt any Captain, Officer, Mariner, or other in the Fleet, to betray his Trust, being convicted of any such Offence by the Sentence of the Court-martial, shall be punished with Death, or such other Punishment as the Nature and Degree of the Offence shall deserve, and the Court-martial shall impose.

VI

of relieving an Enemy

No Person in the Fleet shall relieve an Enemy or Rebel with Money, Victuals, Powder, Shot, Arms, Ammunition, or any other Supplies whatsoever, directly or indirectly, upon Pain of Death, or such other Punishment as the Court-martial shall think fit to impose, and as the Nature and Degree of the Crime shall deserve.

VII

of not sending all Papers found aboard Prize Ships

All the Papers, Charter Parties, Bills of Lading, Passports, and other Writings whatsoever, that shall be taken, seized, or found aboard any Ship or Ships which shall be surprised or taken as Prize, shall be duly preserved, and the very Originals shall, by the Commanding Officer of the Ship which shall take such Prize, be sent entirely, and without Fraud, to the Court of Admiralty, or such other Court of Commissioners, as shall be authorized to determine whether such Prize be lawful Capture, there to be viewed, made use of, and proceeded upon according to Law; upon Pain that every Person offending herein, shall forfeit and lose his Share of the Capture, and shall suffer such further Punishment, as the Nature and Degree of his Offence shall be found to deserve, and the Court-martial shall impose.

VIII

of taking Effects out of any Prize before condemned

No Person in or belonging to the Fleet shall take out of any Prize, or Ship seized for Prize, any Money, Plate, or Goods, unless it shall be necessary, for the better securing thereof, or for the necessary Use and Service of any of his Majesty's Ships or Vessels of War, before the same be adjudged lawful Prize in some Admiralty Court; but the full and entire Account of the whole, without Embezzlement, shall be brought in, and Judgement passed entirely upon the whole without Fraud; upon Pain that every Person offending herein shall forfeit and lose his Share of the Capture, and suffer such further Punishment as shall be imposed by a Court-martial, or such Court of Admiralty, according to the Nature and Degree of the Offence.

IX

of Stripping or ill using Persons taken on board a Prize

If any Ship or Vessel shall be taken as Prize, none of the Officers, Mariners, or other Persons on board her, shall be stripped of their Cloaths, or in any sort pillaged, beaten, or evil-intreated; upon Pain that the Person or Persons so offending, shall be liable to such Punishment as a Court-martial shall think fit to inflict.

X

of not preparing for Fight, and encouraging the Men in time of Action Every Flag Officer, Captain, and Commander in the Fleet, who, upon Signal or Order of Fight, or Sight of any Ship or Ships which it may be his Duty to engage, or who, upon Likelihood of Engagement, shall not make the necessary Preparations for Fight, and shall not in his own Person, and according to his Place, encourage the inferior Officers and Men to fight courageously, shall suffer Death, or such other Punishment, as from the Nature and Degree of the Offence a Court-martial shall deem him to deserve; and if any Person in the Fleet shall treacherously or cowardly yield or cry for Quarter, every Person so offending, and being convicted thereof by the Sentence of a Court-martial, shall suffer Death.

XI

of disobeying Orders in time of Action, &c Every Person in the Fleet, who shall not duly observe the Orders of the Admiral, Flag Officer, Commander of any Squadron or Division, or other his superior Officer, for assailing, joining Battle with, or making Defence against any Fleet, Squadron, or Ship, or shall not obey the Orders of his superior Officer as aforesaid in Time of Action, to the best of his Power, or shall not use all possible Endeavours to put the same effectually in Execution, every such Person so offending, and being convicted thereof by the Sentence of the Court-martial shall suffer Death, or such other Punishment, as from the Nature and Degree of the Offence a Court-martial shall deem him to deserve.

XII

of Cowardice or Neglect of Duty in time of Action Every Person in the Fleet, who through Cowardice, Negligence, or Disaffection, shall in Time of Action withdraw or keep back, or not come into the Fight or Engagement, or shall not do his utmost to take or destroy every Ship which it shall be his Duty to engage, and to assist and relieve all and every of his Majesty's Ships, or those of his Allies, which it shall be his Duty to assist and relieve, every such Person so offending, and being convicted thereof by the Sentence of a Court-martial, shall suffer Death.

XIII

of not pursuing the Enemy, and in time of action not assisting a Friend Every Person in the Fleet, who through Cowardice, Negligence, or Disaffection, shall forbear to pursue the Chace of any Enemy, Pirate, or Rebel, beaten or flying; or shall not relieve or assist a known Friend in View to the utmost of his Power; being convicted of any such Offence by the Sentence of a Court-martial, shall suffer Death.

XIV

of delaying or discouraging the Service on Account of Wages, &c If when Action, or any Service shall be commanded, any Person in the Fleet shall presume to delay or discourage the said Action or Service, upon Pretence of Arrears of Wages, or upon any Pretence whatsoever, every Person so offending, being convicted thereof by the Sentence of the Court-martial, shall suffer Death, or such other Punishment, as from the Nature and Degree of the Offence a Court-martial shall deem him to deserve.

XV

of deserting or running away with Ship or Stores Every Person in or belonging to the Fleet, who shall desert to the Enemy, Pirate, or Rebel, or run away with any of his Majesty's Ships or Vessels of War, or any Ordnance, Ammunition, Stores, or Provision belonging thereto, to the weakening of the Service, or yield up the same cowardly or treacherously to the Enemy, Pirate, or Rebel, being convicted of any such Offence by the Sentence of the Court-martial, shall suffer Death.

XVI

of deserting, or inticing others Every Person in or belonging to the Fleet, who shall desert or intice others so to do, shall suffer Death, or such other Punishment as the Circumstances of the Offence shall deserve, and a Court-martial shall judge fit: And if any Commanding Officer of any of his Majesty's Ships or Vessels of War shall receive or entertain a Deserter from any other of his Majesty's Ships or Vessels, after discovering him to be such Deserter, and shall not with all convenient Speed give Notice to the Captain of the Ship or Vessel to which such Deserter belongs; or if the said Ships or Vessels are at any considerable distance from each other, to the Secretary of the Admiralty, or to the Commander in Chief; every Person so offending, and being convicted thereof by the Sentence of the Court-martial, shall be cashiered.

XVII

of not taking Care of Ships under Convoy The Officers and Seamen of all Ships appointed for Convoy and Guard of Merchant Ships, or of any other, shall diligently attend upon that Charge, without Delay, according to their Instructions in that Behalf; and whosoever shall be faulty therein, and shall not faithfully perform their Duty, and defend the Ships and Goods in their Convoy, without either diverting to other Parts or Occasions, or refusing or neglecting to fight in their Defence, if they be assailed, or running away cowardly, and submitting the Ships in their Convoy to Peril and Hazard; or shall demand or exact any Money or other Reward from any Merchant or Master for convoying of any Ships or Vessels instructed to their Care, or shall misuse the Matters or Mariners thereof; shall be condemned to make Reparation of the Damage to the Merchants, Owners, and others, as the Court of Admiralty shall adjudge, and also be punished criminally according to the Quality of their Offences, be it by Pains of Death or other Punishment, according as shall be adjudged by the Court-martial.

XVIII

of taking Goods on board, other than Gold, Silver, Jewels &c If any Captain, Commander, or other Officer of any of his Majesty's Ships or Vessels, shall receive on board, or permit to be received on board such Ship or Vessel, any Goods or Merchandizes whatsoever, other than for the sole use of the Ship or Vessel, except Gold, Silver, or Jewels, and except the Goods and Merchandizes belonging to any Merchant or other Ship or Vessel which may be shipwrecked, or in imminent Danger of being shipwrecked, either on the High Seas, or in any Port, Creek, or Harbour, in order to the preserving them for their proper Owners, and except such Goods or Merchandizes as he shall at any Time be ordered to take or receive on board by Order of the Lord High Admiral of Great Britain, or the Commissioners for executing the Office of Lord High Admiral for the Time being; every Person so offending, being convicted thereof by the Sentence of the Court-martial, shall be cashiered, and be for ever afterwards rendered incapable to serve in any Place or Office in the Naval Service of his Majesty, his Heirs and Successors.

(The exception of specie was important, for eighteenth-century commerce required international payments to be made in gold or silver in considerable quantities, and it was always safer to ship them in a man-of-war. The captain would charge a commission of 1% or 2%, and might earn considerable sums thereby.)

XIX

of mutinous Assemblies or uttering seditious Words

If any Person in or belonging to the Fleet shall make or endeavour to make any mutinous Assembly upon any Pretence whatsoever, every Person offending herein, and being convicted thereof by the Sentence of the Court-martial, shall suffer Death: And if any Person in or belonging to the Fleet shall utter any Words of Sedition or Mutiny, he shall suffer Death, or such other Punishment as a Court-martial shall deem him to deserve: And if any Officer, Mariner, or Soldier in or belonging to the Fleet, shall behave himself with Contempt to his superior Officer, such superior Officer, being in the Execution of his Office, he shall be punished according to the Nature of his Offence by the Judgment of a Court-martial.

XX

of concealing mutinous Practice or Words

If any Person in the Fleet shall conceal any traiterous or mutinous Practice or Design, being convicted thereof by the Sentence of a Court-martial, he shall suffer Death, or such other Punishment as a Court-martial shall think fit; and if any Person, in or belonging to the Fleet, shall conceal any traiterous or mutinous Words spoken by any, to the Prejudice of his Majesty or Government, or any Words, Practice, or Design, tending to the Hindrance of the Service, and shall not forthwith reveal the same to the Commanding Officer, or being present at any Mutiny or Sedition, shall not use his utmost Endeavours to suppress the same, he shall be punished as a Court-martial shall think he deserves.

XXI

of endeavouring to stir up Disturbance on Account of unwholesomeness of Victual &c

If any Person in the Fleet shall find cause of Complaint of the Unwholesomness of the Victual, or upon other just Ground, he shall quietly make the same known to his Superior or Captain, or Commander in Chief, as the Occasion may deserve, that such present Remedy may be had as the Matter may require; and the said Superior, Captain, or Commander in Chief, shall, as far as he is able, cause the same to be presently remedied; and no Person in the Fleet, upon any such or other Pretence, shall attempt to stir up any Disturbance, upon Pain of such Punishment as a Court-martial shall think fit to inflict, according to the Degree of the Offence.

XXII

of striking, &c a Superior, or disobeying his lawful command

If any Officer, Mariner, Soldier, or other Person in the Fleet, shall strike any of his superior Officers, or draw, or offer to draw, or lift up any Weapon against him, being in the Execution of his Office, on any Pretence whatsoever, every such Person, being convicted of any such Offence by the Sentence of a Court-martial, shall suffer Death; and if any Officer, Mariner, Soldier, or other Person in the Fleet, shall presume to quarrel with any of his superior Officers, being in the Execution of his Office, or shall disobey any lawful Command of any of his superior Officers, every such Person being convicted of any such Offence, by the Sentence of a Court-martial, shall suffer Death, or such other Punishment, as shall, according to the Nature and Degree of his Offence, be inflicted upon him by the Sentence of a Court-martial.

XXIII

of quarrelling, or using reproachful Speeches &c

If any Person in the Fleet shall quarrel or fight with any other Person in the Fleet, or use reproachful or provoking Speeches or Gestures, tending to make any Quarrel or Disturbance, he shall upon being convicted thereof, suffer such Punishment as the Offence shall deserve, and a Court-martial shall impose.

XXIV

of wasting Stores, &c There shall be no wasteful Expence of any Powder, Shot, Ammunition, or other Stores in the Fleet, nor any Embezzlement thereof, but the Stores and Provisions shall be carefully preserved, upon Pain of such Punishment to be inflicted upon the Offenders, Abettors, Buyers, and Receivers (being Persons subject to Naval Discipline) as shall be by a Court-martial found just in that Behalf.

XXV

of burning any Magazine or Vessel, &c not belonging to an Enemy Every Person in the Fleet, who shall unlawfully burn or set Fire to any Magazine or Store of Powder, or Ship, Boat, Ketch, Hoy, or Vessel, or Tackle, or Furniture thereunto belonging, not then appertaining to an Enemy, Pirate, or Rebel, being convicted of any such Offence, by the Sentence of a Court-martial, shall suffer Death.

XXVI

of Neglect in conducting and steering Care shall be taken in the conducting and steering of any of his Majesty's Ships, that through Wilfulness, Negligence, or other Defaults, no Ship be stranded or run upon any Rocks or Sands, or split or hazarded, upon Pain, that such as shall be found guilty therein, be punished by Death, or such other Punishment as the Offence by a Court-martial shall be judged to deserve.

XXVII

of sleeping on Watch, &c No Person in or belonging to the Fleet shall sleep upon his Watch, or negligently perform the Duty imposed on him, or forsake his Station, upon Pain of Death, or such other Punishment as a Court-martial shall think fit to impose, and as the Circumstances of the Case shall require.

XXVIII

of Murder All Murders committed by any Person in the Fleet, shall be punished with Death by the Sentence of a Court-martial.

XXIX

Buggery If any Person in the Fleet shall commit the unnatural and detestable Sin of Buggery or Sodomy with Man or Beast, he shall be punished with Death by the Sentence of a Court-martial.

XXX

Robbery All Robbery committed by any Person in the Fleet, shall be punished with Death, or otherwise, as a Court-martial, upon Consideration of Circumstances, shall find meet.

XXXI

False Musters Every Officer or other Person in the Fleet, who shall knowingly make or sign a false Muster or Muster-book, or who shall command, counsel, or procure the making or signing thereof, or who shall aid or abet any other Person in the making or signing thereof, shall, upon Proof of any such Offence being made before a Court-martial, be cashiered, and rendered incapable of further Employment in his Majesty's Naval Service.

(This was the most common means by which an officer might defraud the public and oppress his own men).

XXXII

not apprehending Prisoners, and permitting Escapes

No Provost-martial belonging to the Fleet shall refuse to apprehend any Criminal, whom he shall be authorized by legal Warrant to apprehend, or to receive or keep any Prisoner committed to his Charge, or wilfully suffer him to escape, being once in his Custody, or dismiss him without lawful Order, upon Pain of such Punishment as a Court-martial shall deem him to deserve: and all Captains, Officers, and others in the Fleet, shall do their Endeavour to detect, apprehend, and bring to Punishment all Offenders, and shall assist the Officers appointed for that Purpose therein, upon Pain of being proceeded against, and punished by a Court-martial, according to the Nature and Degree of the Offence.

XXXIII

scandalous oppressive or fraudulent Behaviour of Officers

If any Flag Officer, Captain or Commander, or Lieutenant belonging to the Fleet, shall be convicted before a Court-martial of behaving in a scandalous, infamous, cruel, oppressive, or fraudulent Manner, unbecoming the Character of an Officer, he shall be dismissed from his Majesty's Service.

(This article may have been added as a result of the court martial in 1742 of Captain the Hon William Hervey, who was dismissed the Service for just such behaviour.)

XXXIV

Mutiny, Desertion or Disobedience on Shore

Every Person being in actual Service and full Pay, and Part of the Crew in or belonging to any of his Majesty's Ships or Vessels of War, who shall be guilty of Mutiny, Desertion, or Disobedience to any lawful Command, in any Part of his Majesty's Dominions on Shore, when in actual Service relative to the Fleet, shall be liable to be tried by a Court-martial, and suffer the like Punishment for every such Offence, as if the same had been committed at Sea on Board any of his Majesty's Ships or Vessels of War.

XXXV

committing on Shore any of the Crimes punishable by these Articles

If any Person who shall be in the actual Service and full Pay of his Majesty's Ships and Vessels of War, shall commit upon the Shore in any Place or Places out of his Majesty's Dominions, any of the Crimes punishable by these Articles and Orders, the Person so offending shall be liable to be tried and punished for the same in like Manner, to all Intents and Purposes, as if the said Crimes had been committed at Sea, on Board any of his Majesty's Ships or Vessels of War.

XXXVI

Other Crimes not Capital, &c to be punished according to the Custom of the Navy

All other Crimes not Capital, committed by any Person or Persons in the Fleet, which are not mentioned in this Act, or for which no Punishment is hereby directed to be inflicted, shall be punished according to the Laws and Customs in such Cases used at Sea.

3 Provided always, That no Person convicted of any Offence shall, by the Sentence of any Court-martial to be held by virtue of this Act, be adjudged to be imprisoned for a longer Term than the Space of two Years.

4 Provided also, That nothing in this Act contained shall extend, or be construed to extend, to impower any Court-martial to be constituted by virtue of this Act, to proceed to the Punishment or Trial of any of the Offences specified in the several Articles contained in this Act, or of any Offence whatsoever (other than the Offences specified in the fifth, thirty-fourth, and thirty-fifth of the foregoing Articles and Orders), which shall not be committed upon the main Sea, or in great Rivers only, beneath the Bridges of the said Rivers nigh to the Sea, or in any Haven, River, or Creek within the Jurisdiction of the Admiralty, and which shall not be committed by such Persons at the Time of the Offence committed shall be in actual Service and full Pay in the Fleet or Ships of War of his Majesty, his Heirs or Successors, such Persons only excepted, and for such Offences only, as are described in the fifth of the foregoing Articles and Orders.

5 Provided also, That nothing in this Act contained shall extend, or be construed to extend, to impower any Court-martial to be constituted by virtue of this Act, to proceed to the Punishment or Trial of any Land Officer or Soldier on Board any Transport Ship, for any of the Offences specified in the several Articles contained in this Act.

6 And it is hereby further enacted, That from and after the twenty-fifth Day of December one thousand seven hundred and forty nine, the Lord High Admiral of Great Britain, or the Commissioners for executing the Office of Lord High Admiral of Great Britain for the Time being, shall have full Power and Authority to grant Commissions to any Officer commanding in Chief any Fleet or Squadron of Ships of War, to call and assemble Courts-martial, consisting of Commanders and Captains; and that in case any Officer commanding in Chief any Fleet or Squadron of Ships of War (who shall be authorized by the Lord High Admiral, or the Commissioners for executing the Office of Lord High Admiral for the Time being, to call and assemble Courts-martial in Foreign Parts) shall happen to die, or be recalled, or removed from his Command, then the Officer upon whom the Command of the said Fleet or Squadron shall devolve, and so, from Time to Time, the Officer who shall have the Command of the Fleet or Squadron, shall have the same Power to call and assemble Courts-martial, as the first Commander in Chief of the said Fleet or Squadron was invested with.

7 Provided always, and it is hereby enacted and declared, That no Commander in Chief of any Fleet or Squadron of his Majesty's Ships, or Detachment thereof, consisting of more than five Ships, shall preside at any Court-martial in Foreign Parts, but that the Officer next in Command to such Officer commanding in Chief, shall hold such Court-martial and preside thereat; any Law, Custom, or Usage to the contrary notwithstanding.

8 And it is hereby further enacted, That from and after the twenty-fifth Day of December one thousand seven hundred and forty-nine, in case any Commander in Chief in any Fleet or Squadron of his Majesty's Ships or Vessels of War in Foreign Parts, shall detach any Part of such Fleet or Squadron, every Commander in Chief shall, and he is hereby authorized and required, by Writing under his Hand, to impower the Chief Commander of the Squadron or Detachment so ordered on such separate Service (and in case of his Death or Removal, the Officer to whom the Command of such separate Squadron or Detachment shall belong) to hold Courts-martial, during the Time of such separate Service, or until the Commander of the said Detachment for the Time being shall return to his Commander in Chief, or shall come under the Command of any other his superior Officer, or return to Great Britain or Ireland.

9 Provided always, and it is hereby further enacted, That if any five or more of his Majesty's Ships or Vessels of War shall happen to meet together in Foreign Parts, then and in such Case, it shall be lawful for the senior Officer of the said Ships or Vessels to hold Courts-martial, and preside thereat, from Time to Time, as there shall be occasion, during so long Time as the said Ships or Vessels of War, or any five or more of them, shall continue together.

10 Provided nevertheless, and be it also enacted, That where any material Objection occurs, which may render it improper for the Person who is next in Command to the senior Officer or Commander in Chief of any Fleet or Squadron of his Majesty's Ships of War in Foreign Parts to hold Courts-martial, or preside thereat, in such Case it shall be lawful for the Lord High Admiral, or Commissioners for executing the Office of Lord High Admiral for the Time being, as also the Commander in Chief of any such Fleet or Squadron of his Majesty's Ships in Foreign Parts, respectively to appoint the third Officer in Command to preside at or hold such Court-martial.

11 And it is hereby further enacted, That from and after the twenty-fifth Day of December one thousand seven hundred and forty-nine, it shall be lawful for the Lord High Admiral of Great Britain, or the Commissioners for executing the Office of Lord High Admiral for the Time being, and they are hereby respectively authorized, from Time to Time, as there shall be Occasion, to direct any Flag Officer, or Captain of any of his Majesty's Ships of War, who shall be in any Port of Great Britain or Ireland, to hold Courts-martial in any such Port, provided such Flag Officer or Captain be the first, second, or third in Command of such Port, as shall be found most expedient, and for the Good of his Majesty's Service; and such Flag Officer or Captain, so directed to hold Courts-martial, shall preside at such Courts-martial; any Thing herein contained to the contrary notwithstanding.

12 And it is hereby further enacted, That from and after the twenty-fifth Day of December one thousand seven hundred and forty-nine, no Court-martial, to be held or appointed by virtue of this present Act, shall consist of more than thirteen, or of less than five Persons, to be composed of such Flag Officers, Captains, or Commanders then and there present, as are next in Seniority to the Officer who presides at the Court-martial.

13 Provided always, and be it enacted by the Authority aforesaid, That nothing herein contained shall extend, or be construed to extend, to authorize or impower the Lord High Admiral, or the Commissioners for executing the Office of Lord High Admiral, or any Officer impowered to order or hold Courts-martial, to direct or ascertain the particular Number of Persons of which any Court-martial, to be held or appointed by virtue of this present Act, shall consist.

14 Provided always, and it is hereby enacted and declared, That in case any Court-martial shall, by virtue of this Act, be appointed to be held at any Place where there are not less than three, nor yet so many as five Officers of the Degree and Denomination of a Post Captain, or of a superior Rank to be found, then it shall be lawful for the Officer, at the Place appointed for holding such Court-martial, who is to preside at the same, to call to his Assistance as many of the Commanders of his Majesty's Vessels, under the Rank and Degree of a Post Captain, as, together with the Post Captains then and there present, will make up the Number of five, to hold such Court-martial.

15 And it is hereby further enacted, That from and after the twenty-fifth Day of December one thousand seven hundred and forty-nine, no Member of any Court-martial, after the Trial is begun, shall go on Shore till Sentence be given, but remain on Board the Ship in which the Court shall first assemble, except in case of Sickness, to be judged of by the Court, upon Pain of being cashiered from his Majesty's Service; nor shall the Proceedings of the said Court be delayed by the Absence of any of its Members, provided a sufficient Number doth remain to compose the said Court, which shall and is hereby required to sit from Day to Day (Sunday always excepted) until the Sentence be given.

16 And it is hereby further enacted, That from and after the twenty-fifth Day of December one thousand seven hundred and forty-nine, upon all Trials of Offenders by any Court-martial, all the Officers present who are to constitute the said Court-martial, shall, before they proceed to such Trial, take such Oath as is herein after-mentioned, upon the Holy Evangelists, before the Court; which Oath the Judge Advocate, or his Deputy, or the Person appointed to officiate as such is hereby authorized and required to administer in the Words following (that is to say),

'I A.B. do swear, That I will duly adminster Justice, according to the Articles and Orders established by an Act passed in the twenty-second Year of the Reign of his Majesty King George the Second, for amending, explaining, and reducing into one Act of Parliament, the Laws relating to the Government of his Majesty's Ships, Vessels, and Forces by Sea, without Partiality, Favour, or Affection; and if any Case shall arise, which is not particularly mentioned in the said Articles and Orders, I will duly administer Justice according to my Conscience, the best of my Understanding, and the Custom of the Navy in the like Cases; and I do further swear, That I will not upon any Account, at any Time whatsoever, disclose or discover the Vote or Opinion of any particular Member of this Court-martial, unless thereunto required by Act of Parliament.

So help me GOD.'

And so soon as the said Oath shall have been administered to the respective members, the President of the Court is hereby authorized and required to administer to the Judge Advocate, or the Person officiating as such, an Oath in the following Words:

'I A.B. do swear, That I will not upon any Account at any Time whatsoever, disclose or discover the Vote or Opinion of any particular Member of the Court-martial, unless thereunto required by Act of Parliament.

So help me GOD.'

17 And it is hereby further enacted, That from and after the twenty-fifth Day of December one thousand seven hundred and forty-nine, in case any Person in the Fleet, being called upon to give Evidence at any Court-martial, shall refuse to give his Evidence upon Oath, or shall prevaricate in his Evidence, or behave with Contempt to the Court, it shall and may be lawful for such Court-martial to punish every such Offender by Imprisonment, at the Discretion of the Court, such Imprisonment not to continue longer than three Months, in case of such Refusal or Prevarication, nor longer than one Month in the Case of such Contempt; and that all and every Person and Persons who shall commit any wilful Perjury, in any Evidence or Examination upon Oath at any such Court-martial, or who shall curruptly procure or subborn any Person to commit such wilful Perjury, shall and may be prosecuted in his Majesty's Court of King's Bench by Indictment or Information; and every Issue joined in any such Inductment or Information shall be tried by good and lawful Men of the County of Middlesex, or such other County as the said Court of King's Bench shall direct; and all and every Person and Persons, being lawfully convicted upon any such Indictment or Information shall be punished with such Pains and Penalties, as are inflicted for the like Offences respectively by two Acts of Parliament, the one made in the fifth Year of the Reign of Queen Elizabeth, intituled, An Act for Punishment of such Persons as shall procure or commit any wilful Perjury; and the other made in the second Year of the Reign of his present Majesty, intituled, An Act for the more effectual preventing and further Punishment of Forgery, Perjury, and Subornation of Perjury, and to make it Felony to steal Bonds, Notes, or other Securities for Payment of Money.

18 And be it further enacted by the Authority aforesaid, That in every Information or Indictment to be prosecuted by virtue of this Act for any such Offence, it shall be sufficient to set forth the Offence charged upon the Defendant without setting forth the Commission or Authority for holding the Court-martial, and without setting forth the particular Matter tried or to be tried, or directed or intended to be tried before such Court.

19 And it is hereby further enacted, That from and after the twenty-fifth Day of December one thousand seven hundred and forty-nine, no Sentence of Death given by any Court martial held within the Narrow Seas (except in Cases of Mutiny) shall be put in Execution till after the Report of the Proceedings of the said Court shall have been made to the Lord High Admiral, or the Commissioners for executing the Office of Lord High Admiral, and his or their Directions shall have been given therein; and if the said Court shall have been held beyond the Narrow Seas, then such Sentence of Death shall not be carried into Execution but by Order of the Commander of the Fleet or Squadron wherein Sentence was passed; and in Cases where Sentence of Death shall be passed in any Squadron, detached from any other Fleet or Squadron upon a separate Service, then such Sentence of Death (except in Cases of Mutiny) shall not be put in Execution, but by Order of the Commander of the Fleet or Squadron, from which such Detachment shall have been made, or of the Lord High Admiral, or Commissioners for executing the Office of Lord High Admiral; and in Cases where Sentence of Death shall be passed in any Court-martial held by the senior Officer of five or more of his Majesty's Ships, which shall happen to meet together in Foreign Parts pursuant to the Power herein before given, then such Sentence of Death (except in Cases of Mutiny) shall not be carried into Execution but by Order of the Lord High Admiral, or Commissioners for executing the Office of Lord High Admiral.

20 And be it further enacted, and declared, That from and after the twenty-fifth Day of December one thousand seven hundred and forty-nine, the Judge Advocate of any Fleet for the Time being, or his Deputy, shall have full Power and Authority, and is hereby required to administer an Oath to any Witness at any Trial by Court-martial; and in the Absence of the Judge Advocate and his Deputy, the Court-martial shall have full Power and Authority to appoint any Person to execute the Office of Judge Advocate.

21 And be it further enacted by the Authority aforesaid, That from and after the twenty-fifth Day of December one thousand seven hundred and forty-nine, all the Powers given by the several Articles and Orders established by this Act, shall remain and be in full Force with respect to the Crews of such of his Majesty's Ships as shall be wrecked, or be otherwise lost or destroyed; and all the Command, Power and Authority given to the Officers of the said Ship or Ships, shall remain and be in full Force as effectually as if such Ship or Ships to which they did belong were not so wrecked, lost or destroyed, until they shall be regularly discharged from his Majesty's further Service, or removed into some other of his Majesty's Ships of War, or until a Court-martial shall be held, pursuant to the Custom of the Navy in such Cases, to enquire into the Causes of the Loss of the said Ship or Ships: And if upon such Enquiry it shall appear by the Sentence of the Court-martial that all, or any of the Officers or Seamen of the said Ship or Ships did their utmost to preserve, get off, or recover the said Ship or Ships, and since the Loss thereof have behaved themselves obediently to their superior Officers, according to the Discipline of the Navy, and the said Articles and Orders herein before established, then all the Pay and Wages of the said Officers and Seamen, or of such of them as shall have done their Duty as aforesaid, shall continue and go on, and be paid to the Time of their Discharge or Death; or if they shall be then alive, to the Time of the holding of such Court-martial, or Removal into some other of his Majesty's Ships of War; and every such Officer and Seaman of any of his Majesty's Ships of War, who after the Wreck or Loss of his Ship shall act contrary to the Discipline of the Navy, and the several Articles and Orders herein before established, or any of them, shall be sentenced by the said Court-martial, and punished as if the Ship to which he did belong was not so wrecked, lost or destroyed.

(The celebrated loss of HMS Wager, one of Anson's squadron, on the coast of Tierra del Fuego in 1741 had drawn attention to the fact that the loss of a ship automatically cancelled her officers' commissions and dissolved all bonds of discipline. This article was intended to prevent any recurrence of the mutinies which had ensued on that occasion. See Peter Shankland, Byron of the Wager [London, 1975].)

22 An be it further enacted, That from and after the said twenty-fifth Day of December one thousand seven hundred and forty-nine, all the Pay and Wages of such Officers and Seamen of any of his Majesty's Ships as are taken by the Enemy, and upon Enquiry at a Court martial shall appear by the Sentence of the said Court to have done their utmost to defend the said Ship or Ships, and since the taking thereof, to have behaved themselves obediently to their superior Officers, according to the Discipline of the Navy, and the said Articles and Orders, herein before established, shall continue and go on, and be paid, from the Time of their being so taken, to the Time of the holding of such Court-martial, or until they shall be regularly discharged from his Majesty's Service, or removed into some other of his Majesty's Ships of War or (if they shall die in Captivity, or not live to the Time of the holding of such Court-martial) to the Time of their Death, in such Manner, and not otherwise, as if the said Ship or Ships to which they did belong respectively, was not or were not so taken.

23 Provided always, and be it further enacted, That no Person or Persons not flying from Justice, shall be tried or punished by any Court-martial for any Offence to be committed against this Act, unless the Complaint of such Offence be made in Writing to the Lord High Admiral, or to the Commissioners for executing the Office of Lord High Admiral for the Time being, or any Commander in Chief of his Majesty's Squadrons or Ships impowered to hold Courts-martial, or unless a Court-martial to try such Offender shall be ordered by the said Lord High Admiral, or the said Commissioners, or the said Commander in Chief, either within three Years after such Offence shall be committed, or within one Year after the Return of the Ship, or of the Squadron, to which such Offender shall belong, into any of the Ports of Great Britain or Ireland; or within one Year after the Return of such Offender into Great Britain or Ireland.

24 And whereas by the said Act, intituled, An Act for the more effectual suppressing of Piracy; it is amongst other Things enacted in the following Words, That the said Captain, Commander, or other Officer of the said Ship or Vessel of War, and all and every the Owners and Proprietors of such Goods and Merchandizes, put on board such Ship or Vessel of War as aforesaid, shall lose, forfeit, and pay the Value of all and every such Goods and Merchandizes so put on board as aforesaid; one Moiety of such full Value to such Person or Persons as shall make the first Discovery, and give Information of or concerning the said Offence; and other Moiety of such full Value to and for the Use of Greenwich Hospital; all of which Forfeitures shall and may be sued for and recovered in the High Court of Admiralty: Now for making the said in part recited Act more useful and effectual, be it enacted by the Authority aforesaid, That from and after the twenty-fifth Day of December one thousand seven hundred and forty-nine, if any Captain, Commander or other Officer of any of his Majesty's Ships or Vessels shall receive on board, or permit or suffer to be received on board such Ship or Vessel, any Goods or Merchandizes, contrary to the true Intent and Meaning of the Eighteenth Article in this Act before-mentioned and hereby enacted, every such Captain, Commander, or other Officer shall, for every such Offence, over and above any Punishment inflicted by this Act, forfeit and pay the Value of all and every such Goods and Merchandizes so received or permitted, or suffered to be received on board as aforesaid, or the Sum of five hundred Pounds of lawful Money of Great Britain, at the Election of the Informer, or Person who shall sue for the same, so that no more than one of these Penalties or Forfeitures shall be sued for and recovered by virtue of this and the said in part recited Act, or either of them, against the same Person, for one and the same Offence, one Moiety of which Penalties or Forfeitures shall be forfeited and paid to the Person who shall inform or sue for the same, and the other Moiety thereof, to and for the Use of the Royal Hospital at Greenwich; which Forfeiture shall be sued for and recovered by Action of Debt, Bill, Plaint, or Information, in any of his Majesty's Courts of Record at Westminister, or in the High Court of Admiralty, at the Election of the Informer or Person who shall sue for the same; and the Court shall award such Costs to the Parties as shall be just; and in all Cases where Judgment or Sentence shall be given against any such Offender, the Court where such Judgment or Sentence shall be given, shall, with all convenient Speed, certify the same to the Lord High Admiral, or to the Commissioners for executing the said Office.

25 Provided always, That nothing in this Act contained, shall extend, or be construed to extend to take away from the Lord High Admiral of Great Britain, or the Commissioners for executing the Office of Lord High Admiral of Great Britain, or any Vice Admiral, or any Judge or Judges of the Admiralty, or his Deputy or Deputies, or any other Officers or Ministers of the Admiralty, or any others having or claiming any Admiral Power, Jurisdiction or Authority within this Realm, or any other the King's Dominions, or from any Person or Court whatsoever, any Power, Right, Jurisdiction, Pre-eminence or Authority, which he or they, or any of them, lawfully hath, have or had, or ought to have and enjoy, before the making of this Act, so as the same Person shall not be punished twice for the same Offence.

26 Provided nevertheless, and be it enacted, That the Repeal of the said before recited Statutes, of any Part thereof, or any Thing herein contained, shall not extend, or be deemed to extend to discharge or avoid, or prevent any Prosecution or Suit commenced, or at any Time hereafter to be commenced against any Person or Persons, for any Offence committed on or before the said twenty-fifth Day of December one thousand seven hundred and forty-nine, or to be committed against the said Statutes, or any Part or Parts thereof, but that all Persons who have been, or shall, before the said twenty-fifth Day of December, be guilty of any such Offence, shall and may be prosecuted, sued, condemned, and punished for the same, as well as after as before the said twenty-fifth Day of December, as if the said Statutes had not been repealed.

Victoria 1866

An Act to make Provision for the Discipline of the Navy
29° and 30° Vic. c.109 (1866)

Whereas it is expedient to amend the Law relating to the Government of the Navy, whereon, under the good Providence of God, the Wealth, Safety, and Strength of the Kingdom chiefly depend:
Be it enacted by the Queen's most Excellent Majesty, by and with the Advice and Consent of the Lords Spiritual and Temporal, and Commons, in this present Parliament assembled, and by the Authority of the same, as follows:

PART I

ARTICLES OF WAR

Public Worship

I

Public Worship to be performed All Officers in Command of Her Majesty's Ships of War shall cause the Public Worship of Almighty God according to the Liturgy of the Church of England established by Law to be solemnly, orderly, and reverently performed in their respective Ships, and shall take care that Prayers and Preaching, by the Chaplains in Holy Orders of the respective Ships, be performed diligently, and that the Lord's Day be observed according to Law.

Misconduct in the Presence of the Enemy

II

Penalty for Misconduct in Action Every Flag Officer, Captain, Commander or Officer commanding subject to this Act who upon Signal of Battle, or on Sight of a Ship of an Enemy which it may be his Duty to engage, shall not,

(1) Use his utmost Exertion to bring his Ship into Action;
(2) Or shall not during such Action, in his own Person and according to his Rank, encourage his Inferior Officers and Men to fight courageously;
(3) Or who shall surrender his Ship to the Enemy when capable of making

a successful Defence, or who in Time of Action shall improperly withdraw from the Fight,

shall, if he has acted traitorously, suffer Death; if he has acted from Cowardice shall suffer Death, or such other Punishment as is herein-after mentioned; and if he has acted from Negligence, or through other Default, he shall be dismissed from Her Majesty's Service, with or without Disgrace, or shall suffer such other Punishment as is herein-after mentioned.

III

Penalty for not pursuing the Enemy and of not assisting a Friend in View

Every Officer subject to this Act who shall forbear to pursue the Chase of any Enemy, Pirate, or Rebel, beaten or flying, or shall not relieve and assist a known Friend in View to the utmost of his Power, or who shall improperly forsake his Station, shall, if he has therein acted traitorously, suffer Death; if he has acted from Cowardice, suffer Death or such other Punishment as is herein-after mentioned; if he has acted from Negligence, or through other Default, shall be dismissed from Her Majesty's Service, with Disgrace, or shall suffer such other Punishment as is herein-after mentioned.

IV

Penalty for delaying or discouraging the Service, or deserting his Post, &c

When any Action or any Service is commanded, every Person subject to this Act who shall presume to delay or discourage the said Action or Service upon any Pretence whatsoever, or in the Presence or Vicinity of the Enemy shall desert his Post or sleep upon his Watch, shall suffer Death or such other Punishment as is herein-after mentioned.

V

Penalty for Misconduct of Subordinate Officers and Men in Action

Every Person subject to this Act, and not being a Commanding Officer, who shall not use his utmost Exertions to carry the Orders of his Superior Officers into execution when ordered to prepare for Action, or during the Action, shall, if he has acted traitorously, suffer Death; if he has acted from Cowardice shall suffer Death, or such other Punishment as is herein-after mentioned; and if he has acted from Negligence, or through other Default, be dismissed from Her Majesty's Service, with Disgrace, or suffer such other Punishment as is herein-after mentioned.

Communications with the Enemy

VI

Penalty for Spies

All Spies for the Enemy shall be deemed to be Persons subject to this Act, and shall suffer Death or such other Punishment as is herein-after mentioned.

VII

Penalty for corresponding, &c with the Enemy

Every Person subject to this Act who shall –

(1) Traitorously hold Correspondence with or shall give Intelligence to the Enemy;

(2) Or Fail to make known to the proper Authorities any Information he may have received from the Enemy;

(3) Or who shall relieve the Enemy with any Supplies,

shall suffer Death, or such other Punishment as is herein-after mentioned.

VIII

Penalty for improper Communication with the Enemy

Every Person subject to this Act who shall, without any treacherous Intention, hold any improper Communication with the Enemy, shall be dismissed with Disgrace from Her Majesty's Service, or shall suffer such other Punishment as is herein-after mentioned.

Neglect of Duty

IX

Penalty for abandoning Post &c

Every Person subject to this Act who shall desert his Post or sleep upon his Watch, or negligently perform the Duty imposed on him, shall be dismissed from Her Majesty's Service, with Disgrace, or shall suffer such other Punishment as is herein-after mentioned.

Mutiny

X

Penalty for Mutiny accompanied by Acts of Violence

Where Mutiny is accompanied by Violence, every Person subject to this Act who shall join therein shall suffer Death, or such other Punishment as is herein-after mentioned; and every Person subject to this Act who shall not use his utmost Exertions to suppress such Mutiny shall, if he has acted traitorously, suffer Death, or such other Punishment as is herein-after mentioned; if he has acted from Cowardice, shall suffer Penal Servitude or such other Punishment as is herein-after mentioned; if he has acted from Negligence he shall be dismissed from Her Majesty's Service, with Disgrace, or suffer such other Punishment as is herein-after mentioned.

XI

Penalty for Mutiny not accompanied by Acts of Violence

Where a Mutiny is not accompanied by Violence, the Ringleader or Ringleaders of such Mutiny shall suffer Death, or such other Punishment as is herein-after mentioned; and all other Persons who shall join in such Mutiny, or shall not use their utmost Exertions to suppress the same, shall suffer Imprisonment or such other Punishment as is herein-after mentioned.

XII

Penalty for inciting to Mutiny

Every Person subject to this Act who shall endeavour to seduce any other Person subject to this Act from his Duty or Allegiance to Her Majesty, or endeavour to incite him to commit any Act of Mutiny, shall suffer Death or such other Punishment as is herein-after mentioned.

XIII

Penalty for Civilians endeavouring to seduce from Allegiance

Every Person, not otherwise subject to this Act, who, being on board any Ship of Her Majesty, shall endeavour to seduce from his Duty or Allegiance to Her Majesty any Person subject to this Act, shall so far as respects such Offence be deemed to be a Person subject to this Act, and shall suffer Death or such other Punishment as is herein-after mentioned.

XIV

Penalty for making mutinous Assemblies or uttering seditious Words

Every Person subject to this Act who shall make or endeavour to make any mutinous Assembly, or shall lead or incite any other Person to join in any mutinous Assembly, or shall utter any Words of Sedition or Mutiny, shall suffer Penal Servitude or such other Punishment as is herein-after mentioned.

XV

Penalty for concealing any traitorous or mutinous Practice, Design, or Words

Every Person subject to this Act who shall wilfully conceal any traitorous or mutinous Practice or Design, or any traitorous or mutinous Words spoken against Her Majesty, or any Words, Practice, or Design tending to the Hindrance of the Service, shall suffer Penal Servitude or such other Punishment as is herein-after mentioned.

XVI

Punishment for striking or attempting to strike, &c superior Officer

Every Person subject to this Act who shall strike, or with any Weapon attempt to strike, or draw or lift up any Weapon against his superior Officer being in the Execution of his Office, shall be punished with Death or such other Punishment as is herein-after mentioned; and every Person subject to this Act who shall, otherwise than with a Weapon, attempt to strike or use or attempt to use any Violence against his superior Officer being in the Execution of his Office, shall be punished with Penal Servitude or such other Punishment as is herein-after mentioned; and every Person subject to this Act who shall strike or attempt to strike, or draw or lift up any Weapon against, or use or attempt to use any Violence against his superior Officer not being in the Execution of his Office, shall be punished with Penal Servitude or such other Punishment as is herein-after mentioned.

Insubordination

XVII

Penalty for Disobedience or using threatening Language to Superior Officer

Every Person subject to this Act who shall wilfully disobey any lawful Command of his superior Officer, or shall use threatening or insulting Language, or behave with Contempt to his Superior Officer, shall be punished with Dismissal with Disgrace from Her Majesty's Service, or suffer such other Punishment as is herein-after mentioned.

XVIII

Penalty for quarrelling, &c, or using reproachful Speech or Gestures

Every Person subject to this Act who shall quarrel or fight with any other Person, whether such other Person be or be not subject to this Act, or shall use reproachful or provoking Speeches or Gestures tending to make any Quarrel or Disturbance, shall suffer Imprisonment or such other Punishment as is herein-after mentioned.

Desertion and Absence without Leave

XIX

Penalty for Desertion

Every Person subject to this Act who shall absent himself from his Ship, or from the Place where his Duty requires him to be, with an Intention of not returning to such Ship or Place, or who shall at any Time and under any Circumstances when absent from his Ship or Place of Duty, do any Act which shows that he has an Intention of not returning to such Ship or Place, shall be deemed to have deserted, and shall be punished accordingly; that is to say,

(1) If he has deserted to the Enemy he shall be punished with Death or such other Punishment as is herein-after mentioned;

(2) If he has deserted under any other Circumstances, he shall be punished with Penal Servitude or such other Punishment as is herein-after mentioned;

and in every such Case he shall forfeit all Pay, Head Money, Bounty, Salvage, Prize Money, and Allowances that have been earned by him, and all Annuities, Pensions, Gratuities, Medals, and Decorations that may have been granted to him, and also all Clothes and Effects which he may have left on board the Ship or at the Place from which he has deserted, unless the Tribunal by which he is tried, or the Admiralty, shall otherwise direct.

XX

Penalty for inducing any Person to desert

Every Person subject to this Act who shall endeavour to seduce any other Person subject to this Act to desert shall suffer Imprisonment or such other Punishment as is herein-after mentioned.

XXI

Penalty for entertaining a Deserter

Every Officer in Command of any Ship of Her Majesty who shall receive or entertain any Deserter from Her Majesty's Military or Naval Forces, after discovering him to be a Deserter, and shall not with all convenient Speed, in the Case of a Deserter from Her Majesty's Naval Forces, give Notice to the Commanding Officer of the Ship to which such Deserter belongs, or, if such Ship is at a Distance, to the Secretary of the Admiralty or to the Commander-in-Chief, or, in case of a Deserter from Her Majesty's Military Forces, give Notice to the Secretary of War, or the Commanding Officer of the Regiment to which such Deserter belongs, the Officer so offending shall be dismissed from Her Majesty's Service, or shall suffer such other Punishment as is herein-after mentioned.

XXII

Punishment for breaking out of Ship

If any Person subject to this Act (without being guilty of Desertion) improperly leaves his Ship or Place of Duty, he shall be liable to Imprisonment or to such other Punishment as is herein-after mentioned, and to such other Punishment by Forfeiture of Wages or of other Benefits as the Admiralty from Time to Time by Regulations prescribe.

XXIII

Penalty for Absence without Leave

Every Person subject to this Act who (without being guilty of Desertion or of improperly leaving his Ship or Place of Duty) shall be absent without Leave shall be liable to Imprisonment for any Period not exceeding Ten Weeks, with or without Hard Labour, or such other Punishment as the Circumstances of the Case may require, and to such other Punishment by Forfeiture of Wages or of other Benefits as the Admiralty from Time to Time by Regulations prescribe.

XXIV

Forfeiture of Effects for Absence without Leave

If any Person subject to this Act is absent without Leave for a Period of One Month (whether he is guilty of Desertion or of improperly leaving his Ship or Place of Duty or not), but is not apprehended and tried for his Offence, he shall be liable to Forfeiture of Wages and other Benefits as the Admiralty from Time to Time by Regulations prescribe, and the Admiralty, or, on a Foreign Station, the Commander-in-Chief, may by an Order containing a Statement of the Absence without Leave direct that the Clothes and Effects (if any) left by him on board Ship or at his Place of Duty be forfeited, and the same may be sold, and the Proceeds of the Sale shall be disposed of as the Admiralty or the Commander-in-Chief (as the Case may be) may direct; and every Order under this Provision for Forfeiture or Sale shall be conclusive as to the Fact of the Absence without Leave as therein stated of the Person therein named; but in any Case the Admiralty may, if it seems fit, on sufficient Cause being shown at any Time after Forfeiture and before Sale, remit the Forfeiture, or after Sale pay or dispose of the Proceeds of the Sale or any Part thereof to or for the Use of the Person to whom the Clothes or Effects belonged, or his Representatives.

XXV

Penalty for assisting, &c Desertion

If any Person not subject to this Act assists or procures any Person subject to this Act to desert or improperly absent himself from his Duty, or conceals, employs, or continues to employ any Person subject to this Act, who is a Deserter or improperly absent from his Duty, knowing him to be a Deserter or so improperly absent, he shall, for every such Offence of Assistance, Procurement, Concealment, Employment, or Continuance of Employment, be liable, on summary Conviction thereof before a Justice or Justices, or before any Person or Persons or Court exercising like Authority in any Part of Her Majesty's Dominions, to a Penalty not exceeding Thirty Pounds; and, notwithstanding anything in any Act relating to Municipal Corporations, or to the Metropolitan Police, or in any other Act, every such Penalty shall be applied as the Admiralty direct.

XXVI

Penalty for persuading to Desertion, &c

If any Person not subject to this Act by Words or otherwise persuades any Person subject to this Act to desert or improperly absent himself from his Duty, he shall for every such Offence be liable, on summary Conviction thereof before a Justice or Justices, or before any Person or Persons or Court exercising like Authority in any Part of Her Majesty's Dominions, to a Penalty not exceeding Twenty Pounds; and, notwithstanding anything in any Act relating to Municipal Corporations, or to the Metropolitan Police, or in any other Act, every such Penalty shall be applied as the Admiralty direct.

Miscellaneous Offences

XXVII

Penalty for profane Swearing and other Immoralities

Every Person subject to this Act who shall be guilty of any profane Oath, Cursing, Execration, Drunkenness, Uncleanness, or other scandalous Action in derogation of God's Honour and Corruption of good Manners, shall be dismissed from Her Majesty's Service, with Disgrace, or suffer such other Punishment as is herein-after mentioned.

XXVIII

Penalty on Officer for Cruelty or Oppression

Every Officer subject to this Act who shall be guilty of Cruelty, or of any scandalous or fraudulent Conduct, shall be dismissed with Disgrace from Her Majesty's Service; and every Officer subject to this Act shall be guilty of any other Conduct unbecoming the Character of an Officer shall be dismissed, with or without Disgrace, from Her Majesty's Service.

XXIX

Penalty for suffering Ships to be improperly lost

Every Person subject to this Act who shall either designedly or negligently or by any Default lose, strand, or hazard, or suffer to be lost, stranded, or hazarded, any Ship of Her Majesty or in Her Majesty's Service, shall be dismissed from Her Majesty's Service, with Disgrace, or suffer such other Punishment as is herein-after mentioned.

XXX

Penalty for not taking care of and defending Ships under Convoy

The Officers of all Ships of Her Majesty appointed for the Convoy and Protection of any Ships or Vessels shall diligently perform their Duty without Delay according to their Instructions in that Behalf; and every Officer who shall fail in his Duty in this respect, and shall not defend the Ships and Goods under his Convoy, without Deviation to any other Objects, or shall refuse to fight in their Defence if they are assailed, or shall cowardly abandon and expose the Ships in his Convoy to Hazard, or shall demand or exact any Money or other Reward from any Merchant or Master for convoying any Ships or Vessels intrusted to his Care, or shall misuse the Masters or Mariners thereof, shall make such Reparation in Damages to the Merchants, Owners, and others as the Court of Admiralty may adjudge, and also shall be punished criminally according to the Nature of his Offence, by Death or such other Punishment as is herein-after mentioned.

XXXI

Master of Merchant Vessel to obey Orders of convoying Officer

Every Master or Other Officer in Command of any Merchant or other Vessel under the Convoy of any Ship of Her Majesty shall obey the Commanding Officer thereof in all Matters relating to the Navigation or Security of the Convoy, and shall take such Precautions for avoiding the Enemy as may be directed by such Commanding Officer; and if he shall fail to obey such Directions, such Commanding Officer may compel Obedience by Force of Arms, without being liable for any Loss of Life or of Property that may result from his using such Force.

XXXII

Penalty for taking any Goods on board other than for the Use of the Vessel except Gold, Silver, Jewels, &c

Every Officer in Command of any of Her Majesty's Ships who shall receive on board or permit to be received on board such Ship any Goods or Merchandises whatsoever, other than for the sole Use of the Ship, except Gold, Silver, or Jewels, and except Goods and Merchandise belonging to any Merchant, or on board any Ship which may be shipwrecked or in imminent Danger either on the High Seas or in some Port, Creek, or Harbour, for the Purpose of preserving them for their proper Owners, or except such Goods or Merchandise as he may at any Time be ordered to take or receive on board by Order of the Admiralty or his Superior Officer, shall be dismissed from Her Majesty's Service, or suffer such other Punishment as is herein-after mentioned.

XXXIII

Penalty for embezzling Public Stores

Every Person subject to this Act who shall wastefully expend, embezzle, or fraudulently buy, sell, or receive any Ammunition, Provisions, or other Public Stores, and every Person subject to this Act, who shall knowingly permit any such wasteful Expenditure, Embezzlement, Sale, or Receipt, shall suffer Imprisonment or such other Punishment as is herein-after mentioned.

XXXIV

Penalty for burning any Magazine or Vessel, &c not belonging to an Enemy

Every Person subject to this Act who shall unlawfully set fire to any Dockyard, Victualling Yard, or Steam Factory Yard, Arsenal, Magazine, Building, Stores, or to any Ship, Vessel, Hoy, Barge, Boat, or other Craft or Furniture thereunto belonging, not being the Property of an Enemy, Pirate, or Rebel, shall suffer Death or such other Punishment as is herein-after mentioned.

XXXV

Penalty for making or signing false Musters

Every Person subject to this Act who shall knowingly make or sign a false Muster or Record or other Official Document, or who shall command, counsel, or procure the making or signing thereof, or who shall aid or abet any other Person in the making or signing thereof, shall be dismissed from Her Majesty's Service, with Disgrace, or suffer such other Punishment as is herein-after mentioned.

XXXVI

Penalty for Misconduct in Hospital

Every Person subject to this Act who shall wilfully do any Act, or wilfully disobey any Orders, whether in Hospital or elsewhere, with Intent to produce or to aggravate any Disease or Infirmity, or to delay his Cure, or who shall feign any Disease, Infirmity, or Inability to perform his Duty, shall suffer Imprisonment or such other Punishment as is herein-after mentioned.

XXXVII

Penalty for endeavouring to stir up any Disturbance on account of Unwholesomeness of the Victuals or other just Grounds

Every Person subject to this Act who shall have any Cause of Complaint, either of the Unwholesomeness of the Victuals or upon any other just Ground, shall quietly make the same known to his Superior, or Captain, or Commander-in-Chief, and the said Superior, Captain, or Commander-in-Chief shall, as far as he is able, cause the same to be presently remedied; and no Person subject to this Act upon any Pretence whatever shall attempt to stir up any Disturbance, upon pain of such Punishment as a Court-martial may think fit to inflict, according to the Degree of Offence.

XXXVIII

Penalty for not sending to the Court of Admiralty all Papers found aboard Prize Ships

All the Papers, Charter-parties, Bills of Lading, Passports, and other Writings whatsoever that shall be taken, seized, or found aboard any Ship or Ships which shall be taken as Prize shall be duly preserved, and the Commanding Officer of the Ship which shall take such Prize shall send the Originals entire and without Fraud to the Court of Admiralty, or such other Court or Commissioners as shall be authorized to determine whether such Prize be lawful Capture, there to be viewed, made use of, and proceeded upon according to Law, upon pain that every Person offending herein shall be dismissed from Her Majesty's Service, or shall suffer such other Punishment as is herein-after mentioned, and in addition thereto shall forfeit and lose his Share of the Capture.

XXXIX

Penalty for taking Money or other Effects out of any Prize before the same shall be condemned

No Person subject to this Act shall take out of any Prize or Ship seized for Prize any Money, Plate, or Goods, unless it shall be necessary for the better securing thereof, or for the necessary Use and Service of any of Her Majesty's Ships and Vessels of War, before the same be adjudged lawful Prize in some Admiralty Court; but the full and entire Account of the whole without Embezzlement shall be brought in, and Judgement passed entirely upon the whole, without Fraud, upon pain that every Person offending herein shall be dismissed from Her Majesty's Service, with Disgrace, or suffer such other Punishment as is herein-after mentioned, and in addition thereto forfeit and lose his Share of the Capture.

XL

Penalty for stripping or ill-using Persons taken on board a Prize

If any Ship or Vessel shall be taken as Prize, none of the Officers, Mariners, or other Persons on board her shall be stripped of their Clothes, or in any sort pillaged, beaten, or evil intreated, upon pain that the Person or Persons so offending shall be dismissed from Her Majesty's Service, with Disgrace, or suffer such other Punishment as is herein-after mentioned.

XLI

Penalty on Commanders capturing as Prize by Collusion, or collusively restoring Ships or Goods

If the Commanding Officer of any of Her Majesty's Ships does any of the following Things, namely,

(1) By Collusion with the Enemy takes as Prize any Vessel, Goods, or Thing;

(2) Unlawfully agrees with any Person for the ransoming of any Vessel, Goods, or Thing taken as Prize; or

(3) In pursuance of any unlawful Agreement for ransoming or otherwise by Collusion actually quits or restores any Vessel, Goods, or Thing taken as Prize;

he shall be liable to Dismissal from Her Majesty's Service, with Disgrace, or to such other Punishment as is herein-after mentioned.

XLII

Penalty for breaking Bulk on board Prize Ship with a View to Embezzlement

If any Person subject to this Act breaks Bulk on board any Vessel taken as Prize, or detained in the Exercise of any Belligerent Right, or under any Act relating to Piracy or to the Slave Trade or to the Customs, with Intent to embezzle anything therein or belonging thereto, he shall be liable to Dismissal from Her Majesty's Service, with Disgrace, or to such other Punishment as is herein-after mentioned, and in addition thereto to forfeit and lose his Share of the Capture.

XLIII

Penalty for Offences against Naval Discipline not particularly mentioned

Every Person subject to this Act who shall be guilty of any Act, Disorder, or Neglect to the Prejudice of good Order and Naval Discipline, not herein-before specified, shall be dismissed from Her Majesty's Service, with Disgrace, or suffer such other Punishment as is herein-after mentioned.

XLIV

Crimes to be punished according to Laws and Customs in use

Any Person subject to this Act committing any Offence against this Act, such Offence not being punishable with Death or Penal Servitude, shall, save where this Act expressly otherwise provides, be proceeded against and punished according to the Laws and Customs in such Cases used at Sea.

Offences punishable by ordinary Law

XLV

Penalty for Offence punishable by ordinary Law

Every Person subject to this Act who shall be guilty of Murder shall suffer Death:

If he shall be guilty of Manslaughter he shall suffer Penal Servitude. or such other Punishment as is herein-after mentioned:

If he shall be guilty of Sodomy with Man or Beast he shall suffer Penal Servitude:

If he shall be guilty of an indecent Assault he shall suffer Penal Servitude or such other Punishment as is herein-after mentioned:

If he shall be guilty of Robbery or Theft he shall suffer Penal Servitude or such other Punishment as is herein-after mentioned:

If he shall be guilty of any other Criminal Offence which if committed in England would be punishable by the Law of England, he shall, whether the Offence be or be not committed in England, be punished either in pursuance of the First Part of this Act as for an Act to the Prejudice of good Order and Naval Discipline not otherwise specified, or the Offender shall be subject to the same Punishment as might for the Time being be awarded by any ordinary Criminal Tribunal competent to try the Offender if the Offence had been committed in England.

XLVI

Offences, when punishable

For all Offences specified or referred to in this Act, if committed by any Person subject thereto in any Harbour, Haven, or Creek, or on any Lake or River, whether in or out of the United Kingdom, or anywhere within the Jurisdiction of the Admiralty, or at any Place on Shore out of the United Kingdom of Great Britain and Ireland, or in any of Her Majesty's Dockyards, Victualling Yards, Steam Factory Yards, or on any Gun Wharf, or in any Arsenal, Barrack, or Hospital belonging to Her Majesty, whether in or out of the said United Kingdom, the Offender may be tried and punished under this Act; and for all Offences herein-before specified under the Headings 'Misconduct in the Presence of the Enemy,' 'Communications with the Enemy,' 'Neglect of Duty,' 'Mutiny,' 'Insubordination,' 'Desertion and Absence without Leave,' or 'Miscellaneous Offences,' if committed by any Person subject to this Act at any Place on Shore, whether in or out of the said United Kingdom, the Offender may be tried and punished under this Act.

PART II

GENERAL PROVISIONS

XLVII

Power of Court-martial to find Intent with which Offence committed

Where the Amount of Punishment for any Offence under this Act depends upon the Intent with which it has been committed, and any Prisoner is charged with having committed such Offence with an Intent involving a greater Degree of Punishment, a Court-martial may find that the Offence was committed with an Intent involving a less Degree of Punishment, and award such Punishment accordingly.

XLVIII

Powers of Court-martial to find Prisoner guilty of lesser Offence on Charge of greater

Where any Prisoner shall be charged with Murder, a Court-martial may find him guilty of Manslaughter or of a Common Assault; where he shall be charged with Sodomy, a Court-martial may find him guilty of an indecent Assault; where he shall be charged with Theft, a Court-martial may find him guilty of an Attempt to thieve, or of Embezzlement, or of wrongful Appropriation of Property belonging to another; and generally where any Prisoner shall be charged with any Offence under this Act he may, upon Failure of Proof of the Commission of the greater Offence, be found guilty of another Offence of the same Class involving a less Degree of Punishment, but not of any Offence involving a greater Degree of Punishment.

XLIX

Rebels and Mutineers to be deemed Enemies

All armed Rebels, armed Mutineers, and Pirates shall be deemed to be Enemies within the Meaning of this Act.

L

Power to arrest Offenders

Every Officer in Command of a Fleet or Squadron of Her Majesty's Ships, or of One of Her Majesty's Ships, or the Senior Officer present at a Port, may, by Warrant under his Hand, authorize any Person to arrest any Offender subject to this Act for any Offence against this Act mentioned in such Warrant; and any such Warrant may include the Names of more Persons than One in respect of several Offences of the same Nature; and any Person named in any such Warrant may forthwith, on his Apprehension, if the Warrant so directs, be taken on board the Ship to which he belongs, or some other of Her Majesty's Ships; and any Person so authorized may use Force, if necessary, for the Purpose of effecting such Apprehension, towards any Person subject to this Act.

LI

Penalty for not assisting in Detection of Prisoners

Every Person subject to this Act who shall not use his utmost Endeavours to detect, apprehend, and bring to Punishment all Offenders against this Act, and shall not assist the Officers appointed for that Purpose, shall suffer Imprisonment or such other Punishment as is herein-after mentioned.

PART III

REGULATIONS AS TO PUNISHMENT

LII

Punishments The following Punishments may be inflicted in Her Majesty's Navy:

(1) Death:
(2) Penal Servitude:
(3) Dismissal with Disgrace from Her Majesty's Service:
(4) Imprisonment or Corporal Punishment:
(5) Dismissal from Her Majesty's Service:
(6) Forfeiture of Seniority as an Officer for a specified Time, or otherwise:
(7) Dismissal from the Ship to which the Offender belongs:
(8) Severe Reprimand, or Reprimand:
(9) Disrating a Subordinate or Petty Officer:
(10) Forfeiture of Pay, Head Money, Bounty, Salvage, Prize Money, and Allowances earned by, and of all Annuities, Pensions, Gratuities, Medals, and Decorations granted to the Offender, or of any One or more of the above Particulars; also, in the Case of Desertion, of all Clothes and Effects left by the Deserter on board the Ship to which he belongs:
(11) Such minor Punishments as are now inflicted according to the Custom of the Navy, or may from Time to Time be allowed by the Admiralty:

And each of the above Punishments shall be deemed to be inferior in Degree to every Punishment preceeding it in the above Scale.

LIII

Regulations as to Infliction of Punishments The following Regulations are hereby made with respect to the Infliction of Punishments in Her Majesty's Navy:

(1) The Admiralty may, except in case of Sentence of Death, which shall only be remitted by Her Majesty, suspend, annul, or modify any Sentence passed on any Person subject to this Act, or substitute a Punishment inferior in Degree for the Punishment involved in any such Sentence, or remit the whole or any Portion of any Punishment into which the Punishment involved in any such Sentence has been commuted, and any Sentence so modified shall (subject to the Provisions of this Act) be valid, and shall be carried into Execution, as if it had been originally passed, with such Modification, by the Court-martial; but so that the Punishment involved in any Sentence be not increased by any such Modification:

(2) Judgment of Death shall not be passed on any Prisoner unless Four at least of the Officers present at the Court-martial, where the Number does not exceed Five, and in other Cases a Majority of not less than Two Thirds of the Officers present, concur in the Sentence:

(3) Except in case of Mutiny, the Punishment of Death shall not be inflicted on any Prisoner until the Sentence has been confirmed by the Admiralty or by the Commander-in-Chief on a Foreign Station:

(4) The Punishment of Penal Servitude may be inflicted for the Term of Life, or for any other Term of not less than Five Years:

(5) The Punishment of Penal Servitude shall in all Cases involve Dismissal with Disgrace from Her Majesty's Service:

(6) A Sentence of Dismissal with Disgrace shall involve in all Cases a Forfeiture of

all Pay, Head Money, Bounty, Salvage, Prize Money, and Allowances that have been earned by, and of all Amenities, Pensions, Gratuities, Medals, and Decorations that may have been granted to the Offender, and an Incapacity to serve Her Majesty again in any Military, Naval, or Civil Service, and may also in all Cases be accompanied by a Sentence of Imprisonment:

(7) The Punishment of Imprisonment may be inflicted for any Term not exceeding Two Years:

(8) A Sentence of Imprisonment may be accompanied with a Direction that the Prisoner shall be kept in Solitary Confinement for any Period of such Term, not exceeding Fourteen Days at any One Time, and not exceeding Eighty-four Days in any One Year, with Intervals between the Periods of Solitary Confinement of not less Duration than the Periods of Solitary Confinement; and when the Imprisonment awarded exceeds Eight-four Days, the Solitary Confinement shall not exceed Seven Days in any Twenty-eight Days of the whole Imprisonment awarded, with Intervals between the Periods of Solitary Confinement of not less Duration than such Periods:

(9) A Sentence of Imprisonment may also be accompanied with a Direction that the Prisoner shall be kept to Hard Labour for all or any Part of the Term of Imprisonment, and Corporal Punishment may be awarded in addition to any Sentence of Imprisonment, whether such Imprisonment is or is not to be accompanied with Solitary Confinement and Hard Labour, or either of them:

(10) The Punishment of Imprisonment, whether on board Ship or on Shore, shall involve disrating in case of a Petty Officer and Reduction to the Ranks in case of a Non-commissioned Officer of Marines, and shall in all Cases be accompanied by Stoppage of Pay or Wages during the Term of Imprisonment:

(11) In any Case of Corporal Punishment not more than Forty-eight Lashes shall be inflicted: No Officer shall be subject to Corporal Punishment; No Petty or Non-commissioned Officer shall be subject to Corporal Punishment, except in case of Mutiny:

All other Punishments authorized by this Act may be inflicted in the Manner heretofore in use in the Navy.

LIV

Limitation of Time as to Trials

No Person, unless he be an Offender who has avoided Apprehension or fled from Justice, shall be tried or punished in pursuance of this Act for any Offence committed by him unless such Trial shall take place within Three Years from the Commission of such Offence, or within One Year after the Return of such Offender to the United Kingdom, where he has been absent from the United Kingdom during such Period of Three Years.

LV

Scale of Punishment

Subject to the foregoing Regulations, where any Punishment is specified by this Act as the Penalty for any Offence, and it is further declared that another Punishment may be awarded in respect of the same Offence, the Expression 'other Punishment' shall be deemed to comprise any One or more of the Punishments inferior in Degree to the specified Punishment, according to the Scale herein-before mentioned; but Corporal Punishment shall be deemed equal in Degree to Imprisonment, and may in all Cases, subject to the foregoing Regulations, be inflicted as a Substitute for or in addition to Imprisonment.

LVI

Authorities having Power to try Officers

Any Offence triable under this Act may be tried and punished by Court-martial; and any Offence triable under this Act, not committed by an Officer (except in the Cases by this Act expressly provided for), and not hereby made Capital, may, under such Regulations as the Admiralty may from Time to Time issue, be summarily tried and punished by the Officer in Command of the Ship to which such Offender belongs, subject to the following Restrictions; (that is to say,)

(1) The Commanding Officer shall not have Power to award the Punishment of Penal Servitude:

(2) The Commanding Officer shall not have Power to sentence a Deserter to Imprisonment for a longer Period than Three Calendar Months, or to sentence any other Offender to Imprisonment for a longer Period than Six Weeks, or to award Solitary Confinement for more than Ten Days at a Time, with Intervals of not less than Seven Days between Two successive Periods of Solitary Confinement:

(3) Except in case of Mutiny, no Man shall be sentenced by the Commanding Officer to Corporal Punishment until his Offence has been inquired into by One or more Officers appointed by such Commanding Officer, and his or their Opinion as to the Guilt or Innocence of the Prisoner reported to such Commanding Officer, and the Commanding Officer shall thereupon act as according to his Judgment may seem right.

LVII

Authorities empowered to impose Punishments to adhere to Provisions herein named

With respect to the Authorities by whom certain Punishments may be imposed, the following Provisions shall take effect; namely,

(1) With respect to any subordinate Officer, the Punishment of Forfeiture of Time or Seniority may be imposed as follows; namely, by the Admiralty for any Time not exceeding Twelve Months, by the Commander-in-Chief on a Foreign Station for any Time not exceeding Six Months, or by the Commanding Officer for any Time not exceeding Three Months:

(2) With respect to any subordinate Officer, the Commander-in-Chief in a Foreign Station shall have Power to impose the Punishments numbered (7), (8), and (9) in the Scale herein-before contained.

PART IV

COURTS-MARTIAL

Constitution of Courts-martial

LVIII

Constitution of Courts-martial

The following Regulations are hereby made with respect to Courts-martial:

(1) A Court-martial shall consist of not less than Five nor more than Nine Officers:

(2) No Officer shall be qualified to sit as a Member of any Court-martial held in pursuance of this Act unless he be a Flag Officer, Captain, Commander, or Lieutenant of Her Majesty's Navy on Full Pay:

(3) A Court-martial shall not be held unless at least Three of Her Majesty's Ships, not being Tenders, and commanded by Captains, Commanders, or Lieutenants of Her Majesty's Navy on Full Pay, are together at the Time when such Court-martial is held:

(4) No Officer shall sit on a Court-martial who is under Twenty-one Years of Age:

(5) No Court-martial for the Trial of a Flag Officer shall be duly constituted unless the President is a Flag Officer, and the other Officers composing the Court are of the Rank of Captain, or of higher Rank:
(6) No Court-martial for the Trial of a Captain in Her Majesty's Navy shall be duly constituted unless the President is a Captain or of higher Rank, and the other Officers composing the Court are Commanders or Officers of higher Rank:
(7) No Court-martial for the Trial of any Person below the Rank of Captain in Her Majesty's Navy shall be duly constituted, unless the President is a Captain or of higher Rank, nor unless in addition to the President there are Two other Members of the Court of the Rank of Commander or of higher Rank:
(8) The Prosecutor shall not sit on any Court-martial for the Trial of a Prisoner whom he prosecutes:
(9) The Admiralty shall have Power to order Courts-martial to be held for the Trial of Offences under this Act, and to grant Commissions to any Officer of Her Majesty's Navy on Full Pay authorizing him to order Courts-martial to be held for the Trial of such Offences:
(10) An Officer holding a Commission from the Admiralty to order Courts-martial shall not be empowered to do so if there is present at the Place where such Court-martial is to be held any Officer superior in Rank to himself, on Full Pay and in command of One or more of Her Majesty's Ships or Vessels, although such last-mentioned Officer may not hold a Commission to order Courts-martial; and in such a Case such last-mentioned Officer may order a Court-martial, although he does not hold any Commission for the Purpose:
(11) If any Officer holding a Commission from the Admiralty to order Courts-martial, having the Command of a Fleet or Squadron, and being in Foreign Parts, die, be recalled, leave his Station, or be removed from his Command, the Officer upon whom the Command of the Fleet or Squadron devolves, and so from Time to Time the Officer who shall have the Command of the Fleet or Squadron, shall, without any Commission from the Admiralty, have the same Power to order Courts-martial as the first-mentioned Officer was invested with:
(12) If any Officer holding a Commission from the Admiralty to order Courts-martial, and having the Command of any Fleet or Squadron of Her Majesty's Ships in Foreign Parts shall detach any Part of such Fleet or Squadron, or separate himself from any Part of such Fleet or Squadron, he may, by Commission under his Hand, empower, in the first-mentioned Case, the Commanding Officer of the Squadron or Detachment ordered on such separate Service, and in case of his Death or ceasing so to command, the Officer to whom the Command of such separate Squadron or Detachment shall belong, and in the secondly-mentioned Case the senior Officer of Her Majesty's Ships on the Division of the Station from which he is absent, to order Courts-martial during the Time of such separate Service, or during his Absence from that Division of the Station (as the Case may be), and every such Authority shall continue in force until revoked, or until the Officer holding it returns to the United Kingdom or until he comes into the Presence of a Superior Officer, empowered to order Courts-martial in the same Squadron, Detachment, or Division of a Station, but so that such Authority shall revive on the Officer holding it ceasing to be in the Presence of such a Superior Officer, and so from Time to Time as often as the Case so requires:
(13) The Officer ordering a Court-martial shall not sit thereon:
(14) The President of every Court-martial shall be named by the Authority ordering the same, or by any Officer empowered by such Authority to name the President:
(15) No Commander or Lieutenant shall be required to sit as a Member of any Court-martial when Four Officers of a higher Rank and junior to the President can

be assembled at the Place where the Court-martial is to be holden (but the Regularity or Validity of any Court-martial or of the Proceedings thereof shall not be affected by any Commander or Lieutenant being required to sit, or sitting, thereon, under any Circumstances); and when any Commander or Lieutenant sits on any Court-martial the Members of it shall not exceed Five in Number:

(16) Subject to the foregoing Regulations, whenever a Court-martial shall be held, the Officer appointed to preside thereat shall summon all the Officers next in Seniority to himself present at the Place where the Court-martial shall be held to sit thereon, until the Number of Nine, or such Number, not less than Five, as is attainable, is complete; subject to this Proviso, that the Admirals and Captains, being Superintendents of Her Majesty's Dockyards, shall not be summoned to sit on Courts-martial unless specially directed to do so by Orders from the Admiralty.

Proceedings of Courts-martial

LIX

Where Courts-martial to be held

A Court-martial under this Act shall be held on board One of Her Majesty's Ships or Vessels of War.

LX

As to Time of Sittings of Courts-martial

A Court-martial held in pursuance of this Act shall sit from Day to Day, with the Exception of Sundays, until Sentence is given, unless prevented from so doing by Stress of Weather or unavoidable Accident, and its Proceedings shall not be delayed by the Absence of any Member, so that not less than Four are present; and no Member shall absent himself unless compelled so to do by Sickness or other just Cause, to be approved of by the other Members of the Court; and if any Member of a Court-martial shall absent himself therefrom, in contravention of this Section, he shall be dismissed from Her Majesty's Service, or shall suffer such other Punishment as may be awarded by a Court-martial.

LXI

Appointment of officiating Judge Advocate

In the Absence of the Judge Advocate of the Fleet or his Deputy, and in default of any Appointment in this Behalf by the Admiralty, or by the Commander-in-Chief of any Fleet or Squadron, the Officer who is to be the President of the Court-martial shall appoint a Person to officiate as Deputy Judge Advocate at the Trial; and the Judge Advocate of the Fleet for the Time being, or his Deputy, or the Person officiating as Deputy Judge Advocate, at any Trial shall administer an Oath to every Witness appearing at the Trial.

LXII

Proceedings at Trial

As soon as the Court is assembled, the Names of the Officers composing the Court shall be read over to the Prisoner, who shall be asked if he objects to being tried by any Member of the Court; if the Prisoner shall object to any Member, the Objection shall be decided by the Court; if the Objection shall be allowed, the Place of the Member objected to shall be filled up by the officer next in Seniority who is not on the Court-martial, subject to the Regulations herein-before contained.

The Prisoner may then raise any other Objection which he desires to make respecting the Constitution of the Court-martial, and the Objection shall then be decided by the Court, which Decision shall be final. and the Constitution of the Court-martial shall not be afterwards impeached, and it shall be deemed to have been in all respects duly constituted.

LXIII

Oaths to be administered to Members of Courts-martial

Before the Court shall proceed to try the Prisoner, the Judge Advocate of the Fleet, or his Deputy, or the Person officiating as Deputy Judge Advocate of the Fleet, shall administer to every Member of the Courts the following Oath; that is to say,

'I do swear, That I will duly administer Justice according to Law, without Partiality, Favour, or Affection; and I do further swear, that I will not on any Account, at any Time whatsoever, disclose or discover the Vote or Opinion of any particular Member of this Court-martial, unless thereunto required in due Course of Law. So help me GOD.'

LXIV

Oath to be administered to Judge Advocate, &c

As soon as the said Oath shall be administered to the Members of the Court-martial, the President shall administer to the Judge Advocate of the Fleet, or his Deputy, or the Person officiating as Deputy Judge Advocate, the following Oath:

'I do swear, That I will not upon any Account, at any Time whatsoever, disclose or discover the Vote or Opinion of any particular Member of the Court-martial, unless thereunto required in due Course of Law. So help me GOD.'

LXV

Power to Admiralty to frame General Orders for Practice of Courts-martial, subject to Approval by Her Majesty in Council

The Admiralty may from Time to Time frame General Orders for altering and regulating (subject to the Provisions of this Act) the Procedure and Practice of Courts-martial under this Act; and any such General Orders shall have full Effect if and when approved by Her Majesty in Council, on a Report of the Judicial Committee of the Privy Council, but not sooner or otherwise; and every Order in Council made under this Section shall be laid before both Houses of Parliament.

LXVI

Summoning Witnesses

Every Person, Civil, Naval, and Military, who may be required to give Evidence before a Court-martial, shall be summoned by Writing under the Hand of One of the Secretaries of the Admiralty, or by the Deputy Judge Advocate, or the Person appointed to officiate as Deputy Judge Advocate at the Trial; and all Persons so summoned and attending as Witnesses before any Court-martial shall, during their necessary Attendance in or on such Court, and in going to and returning from the same, be privileged from Arrest, and shall, if unduly arrested, be discharged by the Court out of which the Writ or Process issued by which such Witness was arrested, or if such Court be not sitting, then by any Judge of the Superior Courts of Westminster or Dublin, or the Court of Session in Scotland, or of the Courts of Law in the East or West Indies or elsewhere, according as the Case shall require, upon its being made to appear to such Court or Judge, by any Affidavit in a summary Way, that such Witness was arrested in going to or returning from or attending upon such Court-martial; and all Witnesses so duly summoned as aforesaid who make default in attending on such Courts, or attending refuse to be sworn or make Affirmation, or being sworn or having made Affirmation refuse to give Evidence, or to answer all such Questions as the Court may legally demand of them, or prevaricate in giving their Evidence, shall upon Certificate thereof under the Hand of the President of such Court-martial, be liable to be attached in the Court of Queen's Bench in London or Dublin, or the Court of Session, or Sheriff Depute or Stewarts Depute, or their respective Substitutes, within their several Shires and Stewartries in Scotland, or Courts of Law in the East or West Indies, or in any of Her Majesty's Colonies, Garrisons, or Dominions in Europe or elsewhere, respectively, upon Complaint made, in like Manner as if such Witness after having been duly summoned and subpoenaed had neglected to attend on a Trial in any Proceeding in the Court in which such Complaint is made, or had refused to be sworn, or on being sworn had refused to give Evidence, or to answer all such Questions as the Court may legally demand, or had prevaricated in giving Evidence, or, if the Court-martial shall think fit, in case any such Person belong to Her Majesty's Navy, being called upon to give Evidence at any Court-martial, shall refuse or neglect to attend to give his Evidence upon Oath or Affirmation, or shall prevaricate in his Evidence, or behave with Contempt to the Court, such Court-martial may punish every such Offender by Imprisonment not longer than Three Months in case of such Refusal, Neglect, or Prevarication, nor longer than One Month in the Case of such Contempt; and every Person not subject to this Act who may be so summoned to attend shall be allowed and paid his reasonable Expenses for such Attendance, under the Authority of the Admiralty, or of the President of the Court-martial on a foreign Station.

LXVII

Penalty on Persons giving false Evidence

Every Person who, upon any Examination upon Oath or upon Affirmation before any Court-martial held in pursuance of this Act, shall wilfully and corruptly give false Evidence, shall be deemed guilty of wilful and corrupt Perjury; and every such Offence, wheresoever committed, shall be triable and punishable in England; and where any such Offence committed out of England is tried in England, all Statutes and Laws applicable to Cases of Perjury shall apply to the Case.

LXVIII

Where Persons are insane at the Time of Offence or Trial

Where it shall appear upon the Trial by Court-martial of any Person charged with an Offence that such Person is insane, the Court shall find specially the Fact of his Insanity, and shall order such Person to be kept in strict Custody in such Place and in such Manner as the Court shall deem fit until the Directions of the Admiralty thereupon are known, and it shall be lawful for the Lords of the Admiralty to give Orders for the safe Custody of such Person during Her Majesty's Pleasure in such Place and in such Manner as they shall think fit.

LXIX

Report of Proceedings of Courts-martial to be transmitted

Every Judge Advocate, or Deputy Judge Advocate, or Person officiating as Deputy Judge Advocate, shall transmit with as much Expedition as may be the original Proceedings, or a complete and authenticated Copy thereof, and the original Sentence of every Court-martial attended by him, to the Commander-in-Chief or senior Officer, who shall transmit them to the Secretary of the Admiralty for the Time being, and any Person tried by a Court-martial shall be entitled, on Demand, to a Copy of such Proceedings and Sentence at any Time not sooner than Six Months after the Trial if the same takes place in the Mediterranean, Three Months if at any other Naval Station within Europe, and Twelve Months if elsewhere, (upon Payment for the same at the Rate of Fourpence per Folio of Seventy-two Words,) but no such Demand shall be allowed after the Space of Three Years from the Date of the final Decision of such Court.

PART V

PENAL SERVITUDE AND PRISONS

Penal Servitude

LXX

Sentence of Penal Servitude

Whenever any Sentence of Death shall be commuted for Penal Servitude, or whenever Sentence of Penal Servitude shall be passed upon any Offender by any Court-martial, and such Sentence, or any Part thereof, is intended to be carried into effect, the Admiralty shall cause the same to be notified in Writing to any Justice of the Queen's Bench, Common Pleas, or Baron of the Exchequer, and thereupon such Justice or Baron shall make an Order for the Penal Servitude of such Offender upon the Terms and for the Time specified in such Notification, and shall do all such other Acts consequent upon such Notification, as any such Justice or Baron is or may be authorized to make or do by any Statute or Statutes in force at the Time of making any such Order in relation to Penal Servitude of Offenders sentenced by Courts of Criminal Jurisdiction to Penal Servitude; and such Order and other Acts to be so made and done as aforesaid shall be obeyed and executed by such Person in whose Custody such Offender may at that Time be, and by all other Persons whom it may concern, and shall be as effectual and have all the same Consequences as any Order made under the Authority of any Statute relating to Penal Servitude with respect to any Offender in such Statute mentioned; and every Sheriff, Gaoler, Keeper, Governor, or Superintendent whom it may concern, and all Constables and other Persons, shall be bound to obey the aforesaid Order and Orders, and be assistant in the Execution thereof, and be liable to the same Punishment for Disobedience to or for interrupting the Execution of such Order as they would be if the same had been made under the Authority of any such Statute; and every Person so ordered to be kept in Penal Servitude shall be subject to all the Penalties and Provisions made by Law, and in force for the Time being, concerning Persons under Sentence of Penal Servitude, or receiving Her Majesty's Pardon on Condition of Penal Servitude; and from the Time when such Order of Penal Servitude is made, every Law in force touching the Escape of Felons, or their afterwards returning or being at large without Leave, shall apply to such Offender, and to all Persons aiding, abetting, contriving, or assisting in any Escape or intended Escape, or the returning without Leave of any such Offender; and the Judge or Baron who makes an Order for Penal Servitude as aforesaid shall direct the Notification of the Admiralty, and his own Order made thereupon, to be filed and kept of Record in the Office of the Clerk of the Crown of the Court of Queen's Bench, and the said Clerk shall have a Fee of Two Shillings and Sixpence only for filing the same, and shall, on Application, deliver a Certificate in Writing (not taking more than Two Shillings and Sixpence for the same) to such Offender, or to any Person applying in his or the Admiralty's Behalf, showing the Christian and Surname of such Offender, his Offence, the Place where the Court was held before which he was convicted, the Sentence, and the Conditions on which the Order of Penal Servitude was made, and such Certificate shall be sufficient Proof of the Conviction and of the Sentence of such Offender, and also of the Terms on which such Order for his Penal Servitude was made, in any Court and in any Proceeding wherein it may be necessary to inquire into the same.

LXXI

Disposal of Offender after Sentence of Penal Servitude When any Sentence of Death shall have been commuted for Penal Servitude, or when any Person subject to this Act shall have been condemned to Penal Servitude, it shall be lawful for the Admiralty, or any Commander-in-Chief on any Foreign Station, or the Commanding Officer of the Ship to which such Person belongs or has belonged, to cause him to be detained and conveyed to any One of Her Majesty's Ships, or any Goal or Prison, there to remain in safe Custody until he is removed therefrom by the Order of the Admiralty or any such Commander-in-Chief or other due Authority, or under an Order for his Penal Servitude, to be made by some Justice of the Queen's Bench or Common Pleas or Baron of the Exchequer as aforesaid, and a Certificate of his Sentence (such Certificate to be signed by the Secretary of the Admiralty, or by any such Commander-in-Chief, or such Commanding Officer) shall be a sufficient Authority to the Commanding Officer of the Ship to which he may be sent, or to the Governor, Keeper, or Superintendent of the Gaol or Prison, to receive and detain him.

LXXII

Subsistence of Offender In case any such Offender shall be conveyed to any Prison, not being a Naval Prison appointed by virtue of this Act, an Allowance such as the Admiralty shall from Time to Time direct shall be made to the Governor, Keeper, or Superintendent of the Gaol or Prison for the Subsistence of such Offender during his Detention therein, and such Allowance shall be paid by Order of the Admiralty upon Production by the said Governor, Keeper, or Superintendent of a Declaration, to be made by him before One of Her Majesty's Justices of the Peace of such County, of the Number of Days during which the Offender has been so detained and subsisted in such Gaol or Prison.

LXXIII

Imprisonment of Offender already under Sentence for previous Offence Whenever Sentence shall be passed by a Court-martial on an Offender already under Sentence either of Imprisonment or of Penal Servitude, passed upon him by a Court-martial for a former Offence, the Court may award Sentence of Imprisonment or Penal Servitude for the Offence for which he is under Trial to commence at the Expiration of the Imprisonment or Penal Servitude to which he has been previously sentenced, although the aggregate of the Terms of Imprisonment or Penal Servitude may exceed the Term for which either of those Punishments could be otherwise awarded.

Prisons

LXXIV

Terms and Place of Imprisonment Every Term of Penal Servitude or of Imprisonment in pursuance of this Act shall be reckoned as commencing on the Day on which the Sentence was awarded, and the Place of Imprisonment, whether the Imprisonment was awarded as an original or as a commuted Punishment, shall be such Place as may be appointed by the Court or the Commanding Officer awarding the Punishment, or which may from Time to Time be appointed by the Admiralty, or by the Commander-in-Chief or senior Officer present on any Foreign Station, and may be One of the Naval Prisons appointed under this Act, or any Common Gaol, House of Correction, or Military Prison within Her Majesty's Dominions.

LXXV

Place of Imprisonment may be changed, &c

Whenever it is deemed expedient it shall be lawful for the Admiralty or any such Commander-in-Chief, by any Order in Writing, from Time to Time to change the Place of Confinement of any Offender imprisoned or sentenced to be imprisoned or detained in pursuance of this Act, and the Gaoler or other Person having the Custody of such Offender shall immediately on the Receipt of such Order remove such Offender to the Gaol, Prison, or House of Correction mentioned in the said Order, or shall deliver him over to Naval Custody for the Purpose of the Offender being removed to such Prison; and every Gaoler or Keeper of such last-mentioned Prison, Gaol, or House of Correction shall, upon being furnished with a Copy of such Order of Removal, attested by the Secretary of the Admiralty for the Time being, receive into his Custody and shall confine pursuant to such Sentence or Order every such Offender.

LXXVI

Expenses of Removal or Subsistence of Prisoners

The Gaoler or other Person removing any Offender in pursuance of such Order shall be allowed for the Charges of such Removal a Sum not exceeding One Shilling a Mile, and when any Offender is not confined in a Naval Prison the Gaoler or other Person in whose Custody any such Offender may be shall receive such an Allowance as the Admiralty shall from Time to Time direct for every Day that such Offender is in his Custody, to be applied towards his Subsistence, and such Sum shall be paid to the said Gaoler or other Person under the Authority of the Admiralty, upon the Application in Writing made to the Secretary of the Admiralty by any Justice for the County or Place in which such Gaol, Prison, or House of Correction shall be situate, with a Copy of the Sentence or Order under which the Prisoner is confined.

LXXVII

Delivery of Prisoners

From and after the passing of this Act, Section One of the Act of the Forty-fourth Year of the Reign of King George the Third (Chapter Thirteen). 'to prevent the Desertion and Escape of Petty Officers, Seamen, and others from His Majesty's Service by Means or under Colour of any Civil or Criminal Process,' shall be read and have effect as if the Words 'One Shilling' were therein substituted for the Words 'Two Shillings;' and any such Sheriff, Gaoler or other Officer as therein mentioned shall, if required, deliver such Petty Officer, Seaman, or other Person as therein mentioned to any Person authorized to receive him, instead of conducting and conveying him as therein provided.

LXXVIII

Proviso for Discharge or Removal of Prisoners

Whenever any Prisoner is undergoing Imprisonment in pursuance of this Act, it shall be lawful for the Admiralty, or any Commander-in-Chief on any Foreign Station, or where an Offender has been imprisoned by Order of his Commanding Officer, for such Commanding Officer or the Admiralty, or any such Commander-in-Chief, to give an Order in Writing directing that the Prisoner be discharged; and it shall also be lawful for the Admiralty, or any such Commander-in-Chief, and any Officer commanding any of Her Majesty's Ships, by Order in Writing, to direct that any such Prisoner be delivered over to Naval Custody for the Purpose of being brought before a Court-martial, either as a Witness, or for Trial or otherwise, and such Prisoner shall accordingly, on the Production of any such Order, be discharged, or be delivered over to such Custody.

LXXIX

Proviso as to Time of Detention in Naval Custody

The Time during which any Prisoner under Sentence of Imprisonment is detained in Naval Custody shall be reckoned as Imprisonment under his Sentence for whatever Purpose such Detention takes place; and the Governor, Gaoler, Keeper, or Superintendent who shall deliver over any such Prisoner shall again receive him from Naval Custody, so that he may undergo the Remainder of his Punishment.

LXXX

In case of Insanity Prisoners to be removed to some Lunatic Asylum

If any Person imprisoned by virtue of this Act shall become insane, and a Certificate to that Effect shall be given by Two Physicians or Surgeons, the Admiralty shall, by Warrant, direct the Removal of such Person to such Lunatic Asylum or other proper Receptacle for insane Persons in the United Kingdom as they may judge proper for the unexpired Term of his Imprisonment; and if any such Person shall in the same Manner be certified to be again of sound Mind, the Admiralty may issue a Warrant for his being removed to such Prison or Place of Confinement as may be deemed expedient, to undergo the Remainder of his Punishment, and every Gaoler or Keeper of any Prison, Gaol, or House of Correction shall receive him accordingly.

LXXXI

Admiralty may set apart Buildings and Ships as Naval Prisons

The Admiralty may set apart any Buildings or Vessels, or any Parts thereof, as Naval Prisons, and any Buildings or Vessels or Parts of Buildings or Vessels, so set apart shall be deemed to be Naval Prisons within the Meaning of this Act, and all Powers and Authorities with respect to County Gaols or Houses of Correction which now are or which may hereafter be vested in any of Her Majesty's Principal Secretaries of State shall, with respect to all such Naval Prisons, belong to the Admiralty; and it shall be lawful for the Admiralty from Time to Time to make, alter, and repeat Regulations for the Government and Superintendence of any such Naval Prison, and of the Officers and Servants thereof, and of Offenders confined therein, and from Time to Time to appoint Inspectors and all other necessary Officers and Servants for any such Naval Prison, and, as Occasion may arise, to remove the Inspectors, Officers, or Servants of any such Naval Prison; and the senior Officer at any Port or Place or on any Station where there may be any such Naval Prison, or such senior Officer and such other Person and Persons as the Admiralty may from Time to Time appoint, shall be a Visitor or Visitors of such Prison; and every Inspector, Visitor, or Officer having the Charge or Command of any such Naval Prison respectively shall, subject to such Rules and Regulations as may from Time to Time be made as aforesaid, have and exercise, in respect of such Prison, and of the Officers and Servants thereof, and of the Prisoners confined therein, all the Powers and Authorities as well in respect of administering Oaths as otherwise which any Inspector, Visiting Justice, or Governor of a County Gaol or House of Correction may respectively exercise as such.

LXXXII

Penalties on aiding Escape or Attempt to escape of Prisoners and on Breach of Prison Regulations

If any Person shall convey or cause to be conveyed into any such Naval Prison any Arms, Tools, or Instruments, or any Mask or other Disguise, to facilitate the Escape of any Prisoner, or by any Means whatever shall aid any Prisoner to escape or in an Attempt to escape from such Prison, whether an Escape be actually made or not, such Person shall be deemed guilty of Felony, and upon being convicted thereof shall be imprisoned, with or without Hard Labour, for any Term not exceeding Two Years, or suffer Penal Servitude for any Term not exceeding Fourteen Years; and if any Person shall bring or attempt to bring into such Prison, in contravention of the Rules, any spirituous or fermented Liquor, he shall for every such Offence be liable to a Penalty not exceeding Twenty Pounds and not less than Ten Pounds; and if any Person shall bring into such Prison, or to or for any Prisoner, without the Knowledge of the Officer having Charge or Command thereof, any Money, Clothing, Provisions, Tobacco, Letters, Papers, or other Articles not allowed by the Rules of the Prison to be in the Possession of a Prisoner, or shall throw into the said Prison any such Articles, or by Desire of any Prisoner, without the Sanction of the said Officer, shall carry out of the Prison any of the Articles aforesaid, he shall for every such Offence be liable to a Penalty not exceeding Five Pounds; and if any Person shall interrupt any Officer of such Prison in the Execution of his Duty, or shall aid or excite any Person to assault, resist, or interrupt any such Officer, he shall for every such Offence be liable to a Penalty not exceeding Five Pounds, or if the Offender be a Prisoner, he shall, upon Conviction thereof before Two Justices of the Peace, or not less than Three of the Visitors of the Prison, be liable to be sentenced for every such Offence to be imprisoned, either with or without Hard Labour, and with or without Solitary Confinement, for any Time not exceeding Six Calendar Months, in addition to so much of the Time for which he was originally sentenced as may be then unexpired, and every Penalty which may be incurred under this Section shall be recoverable in a summary Manner; and such Two Justices or Three Visitors are hereby authorized to issue Warrants of Distress and Sale of the Offender's Goods, and every such Penalty shall be applied as the Admiralty shall direct, any Law, Statute, Charter, or Custom to the contrary notwithstanding.

LXXXIII

Penalty as regards Gaolers, &c

Every Governor, Gaoler, and Keeper of any Prison, Gaol, or House of Correction, and every Officer having the Charge or Command of any Place, Ship, or Vessel for Imprisonment, who shall, without lawful Excuse, refuse or neglect to receive or confine, remove, discharge, or deliver up any Offender against the Provisions of this Act, or any of them, shall incur for every such Refusal or Neglect a Penalty not exceeding One hundred Pounds to be recovered in a summary Manner before Two Justices of the Peace; and such Two Justices are hereby authorized to issue Warrants of Distress and Sale of the Offender's Goods, and every such Penalty shall be applied as the Admiralty shall direct, any Law, Statute, Charter, or Custom to the contrary notwithstanding.

PART VI

SUPPLEMENTAL PROVISIONS

LXXXIV

Short Title

This Act may be cited for all Purposes as The Naval Discipline Act, 1866.

LXXXV

Commencement of Act

Except as otherwise provided, this Act shall be in force within the United Kingdom; and as regards the United Kingdom the Enactments described in the Schedule to this Act shall be repealed from and after One Calendar Month from the passing hereof; and as regards elsewhere this Act shall be in force, and the said Enactments shall be repealed, from and after Six Calendar Months from the passing hereof.

LXXXVI

Definition of Terms In the Construction of this Act, unless there be something in the Context or Subject Matter repugnant to or inconsistent with such Construction, 'Admiralty,' or 'the Lords of the Admiralty,' shall mean the Lord High Admiral for the Time being of the United Kingdom of Great Britain and Ireland, and when there shall be no such Lord High Admiral in Office, any Two or more of the Commissioners for executing the Office of Lord High Admiral of the United Kingdom:

'Officer' shall mean an Officer belonging to One of Her Majesty's Ships, and shall include a subordinate and a Warrant Officer, but shall not extend to Petty and Non-commissioned Officers:

When the Words 'Superior Officer' are used in this Act they shall be held to include all Officers, including Petty and Non-commissioned Officers.

LXXXVII

Persons subject to this Act Every Person in or belonging to Her Majesty's Navy, and borne on the Books of any One of Her Majesty's Ships in Commission, shall be subject to this Act; and all other Persons hereby made liable thereto shall be triable and punishable under the Provisions of this Act.

LXXXVIII

Land Forces embarked as Passengers Her Majesty's Land Forces, when embarked on board any of Her Majesty's Ships, shall be subject to the Provisions of this Act to such Extent and under such Regulations as Her Majesty, Her Heirs and Successors, by any Order or Orders in Council, shall at any Time or Times direct.

LXXXIX

Other Persons embarked as Passengers All other Persons ordered to be received or being Passengers on board any of Her Majesty's Ships shall be deemed to be Persons subject to this Act, under such Regulations as the Admiralty may from Time to Time direct.

XC

Provisions respecting Discipline in hired Ships in Her Majesty's Service in War With respect to hired Vessels in Her Majesty's Service in Time of War, being either armed or under the Command of an Officer in Her Majesty's Naval Service, the following Provisions shall take effect if in any Case the Admiralty think fit so to direct, and where such Direction is given the same shall be specified in the Ship's Articles:

(1) Every Person borne on the Books of any such hired Vessel shall be subject to this Act:

(2) Any Offence committed by any such Person shall be tried and punished as the like Offence might be tried and punished if committed by any Person in or belonging to Her Majesty's Navy, and borne on the Books of any of Her Majesty's Ships in Commission:

(3) Every such Offender who is to be tried by Court-martial shall be placed under all necessary Restraint until he can be tried by Court-martial:

(4) On Application made to the Lords of the Admiralty, or to the Commander-in-Chief, or senior Officer of any of Her Majesty's Ships or Vessels of War abroad authorized to assemble and hold Courts-martial, the Lords of the Admiralty, Commander-in-Chief, or senior Officer (as the Case may be) shall assemble and hold a Court-martial for the Trial of the Offender:

(5) The Officer commanding every such hired Vessel shall have the same Power in respect of all other Persons borne on the Books thereof, or for the Time being on board the same, as the Officer commanding One of Her Majesty's Ships has for the Time being in respect of the Officers and Crew thereof or other Persons on board the same:

(6) The Naval Commander-in-Chief and senior Naval Officer in Her Majesty's Service shall have the same Powers over the Officers and Crew of every such hired Vessel as they have for the Time being over the Officers and Crew of any of Her Majesty's Ships.

XCI

Crews of Ships lost or destroyed

When any One of Her Majesty's Ships shall be wrecked or lost or destroyed, or taken by the Enemy, such Ship shall, for the Purposes of this Act, be deemed to remain in Commission until her Crew shall be regularly removed into some other of Her Majesty's Ships of War, or until a Court-martial shall have been held, pursuant to the Custom of the Navy in such Cases, to inquire into the Cause of the Wreck, Loss, Destruction, or Capture of the said Ship.

XCII

All the Officers and Crew of lost Ship may be tried by One Court

When no specific Charge shall be made against any Officer or Seaman or other Person in the Fleet for or in respect or in consequence of such Wreck, Loss, Destruction, or Capture, it shall be lawful to try all the Officers and Crew or all the surviving Officers and Crew of any such Ship, together, before One and the same Court, and to call upon all or any of them when upon their Trial to give Evidence on Oath or Affirmation before the Court touching any of the Matters then under Inquiry, but no Officer or Seaman or other Person shall be obliged to give any Evidence which may tend to criminate himself.

XCIII

or by separate Courts

When deemed necessary by the Admiralty, or any Officer authorized to order Courts-martial, separate Courts-martial shall be held for the Trial of some One or more of such Officers and Crew for in respect or in consequence of the Wreck, Loss, Destruction, or Capture of any such Ship.

XCIV

For subsequent Offence, separate Court

For any Offence or Offences committed by any Officer or Seaman, or Officers and Seamen, after the Wreck, Loss, Destruction, or Capture of any such Ship, a separate Court-martial shall be held for the Trial of such Offender or Offenders.

XCV

Pay of Crews of Ships lost or taken

When any Ship of Her Majesty shall be wrecked, lost, or otherwise destroyed, or taken by the Enemy, if it shall appear by the Sentence of a Court-martial that the Crew of such Ship did, in the Case of a Ship wrecked or lost, do their utmost to save her or get her off, and in the Case of a Ship taken by the Enemy did their utmost to defend themselves, and that they have, since the Wreck, Destruction, Loss or Capture of such Ship, behaved themselves well, and been obedient to their Officers, then all the Pay of such Crews, or of such Portions of such Crews as have behaved themselves well and been obedient to their Officers, shall be continued until the Time of their being discharged or removed into other Ships of Her Majesty, or dying.

XCVI

When Ship of senior Officer is lost he may dispose of Officers and Crew of lost Ship

If the Ship of any Officer ordered to command any Two or more of Her Majesty's Ships shall be wrecked, lost, or otherwise destroyed, such Officer shall continue in the Command of any Ship or Ships which at the Time of his Ship being wrecked, lost, or destroyed was or were under his Command, and it shall be lawful for such Officer to order the surviving Officers and Crew of the wrecked, lost, or destroyed Ship to join any other Ship under his Command, or to distribute them among the other Ships under his Command, if more than One, and such Officer shall, until he meets with some other Officer senior to himself, have the same Power and Authority in all respect as if his Ship had not been wrecked, lost, or destroyed.

XCVII

Restriction on Arrest of Seamen, &c for Debt

It shall not be lawful for any Person to arrest any Petty Officer or Seaman, Non-commissioned Officer of Marines or Marine, belonging to any Ship of Her Majesty, by any Warrant, Process, or Writ issued in any Part of Her Majesty's Dominions for any Debt, unless the Debt was contracted at a Time when the Debtor did not belong to Her Majesty's Service, nor unless before the issuing of the Warrant, Process, or Writ the Plaintiff in the Suit or some Person on his Behalf has made an Affidavit in the Court out of which it issued that the Debt justly due to the Plaintiff (over and above all Costs) was contracted at a Time when the Debtor did not belong to Her Majesty's Service, nor unless a Memorandum of such Affidavit is marked on the Back of the Warrant, Process, or Writ.

XCVIII

Discharge from Arrest

If any Petty Officer or Seaman, Non-commissioned Officer of Marines or Marine, is arrested in contravention of the Provisions of the last foregoing Section, the Court out of which the Warrant, Process, or Writ issues, or any Judge thereof, may, on Complaint by the Party arrested, or by his superior Officer, investigate the Case on Oath or otherwise, and if satisfied that the Arrest was made in contravention of the Provisions of the last foregoing Section, may make an Order for the immediate Discharge of the Party arrested, without Fee, and may award to the Complainant the Costs of his Complaint, to be taxed by the proper Officer, for the Recovery whereof he shall have the like Remedy as the Plaintiff in the Suit would have on Judgment being given in his Favour, with Costs.

PART VII

SAVING CLAUSE

XCIX

Trial of Offences against repealed Acts

Any Person who has committed or may commit, before this Act comes into force, any Offence against The Naval Discipline Act, 1864, or the Act thereby repealed, or against any other Enactment repealed by this Act, for which such Person has not been tried before this Act comes into force, shall be tried and punished under this Act as if such Crime or Offence had been committed against the same, but he shall not suffer any greater Punishment than he was liable to under The Naval Discipline Act, 1864, or the Act thereby repealed, or such other Enactment (as the Case may be); and any Proceeding of any Court-martial, or any other Proceedings under The Naval Discipline Act, 1864, or such other Enactment which may be pending when this Act comes into force, shall be continued, and the Offender, if found guilty, shall be punished as if the Act or Enactment against which he offended had not been repealed.

C

Nothing to take away Prerogative of the Crown, or Rights or Powers of Admiralty

Nothing in this Act shall take away, abridge, or control further or otherwise than as expressly provided by this Act, any Right, Power, or Prerogative of Her Majesty the Queen in right of Her Crown, or in right of Her Office of Admiralty or any Right or Power of the Admiralty.

CI

Act not to supersede Authority of ordinary Courts

Nothing in this Act contained shall be deemed or taken to supersede or affect the Authority or Power of any Court or Tribunal of Ordinary Civil or Criminal Jurisdiction, or any Officer thereof, in Her Majesty's Dominions, in respect of any Offence mentioned in this Act which may be punishable or cognizable by the Common or Statute Law, or to prevent any Person being proceeded against and punished in respect of any such Offence otherwise than under this Act.

Further reading

D A Baugh, ed, *Naval Administration 1715-50* (Navy Records Society Vol CXX, 1977)

J S Corbett, ed, *Fighting Instructions 1530-1816* (N R S XXIX, 1909)

D Erskine, ed, *Augustus Hervey's Journal* (London, 1953)
Hervey was one of the leaders of the opposition to the 1749 Naval Bill.

S R Gardiner & C T Atkinson, eds, *Letters and Papers relating to the First Dutch War, 1652-1654, Vol III* (N R S XXX, 1906)
Prints on p 293 the text of the 1652 regulations.

C Gill, *The Naval Mutinies of 1797* (Manchester, 1913)

L G Carr Laughton, 'The Preamble to the Articles of War', *The Mariner's Mirror* Vol VII p 82

C C Lloyd, 'The Preamble to the Articles of War', *ibid* XLIII, p 330

G E Manwaring & B Dobrée, *The Floating Republic* (London, 1935)
Another account of the mutinies of 1797.

M Oppenheim, *A History of the Administration of the Royal Navy to 1660* (London, 1896)

Dudley Pope, *At 12 Mr Byng was Shot* (London, 1967)

E L Rasor, *Reform in the Royal Navy; A Social History of the Lower Deck 1850-1880* (Hamden, Connecticut, 1976)

H W Richmond, ed, *Papers relating to the Loss of Minorca in 1756* (N R S XLII, 1913)

idem, The Navy in the War of 1739-48 (Cambridge, 1920)
Deals with the Battle of Toulon and the resultant courts martial.

N A M Rodger, *The Admiralty* (Lavenham, Suffolk, 1979)